The Poetry of Wilfred Owen

The Poetry of Wilfred Owen

This edition published in 2020 by Arcturus Publishing Limited
26/27 Bickels Yard, 151–153 Bermondsey Street,
London SE1 3HA

AD007502UK

Printed in the UK

MIX
Paper from responsible sources
FSC® C018072
FSC www.fsc.org

Contents

Introduction

Born in Oswestry, near the Welsh border, in 1893, Wilfred Owen was the typical product of a middle-class family in the late-Victorian era. A serious boy, he worked hard at his studies and developed a particular interest in botany and geology. On Sundays, he was preoccupied with religion, a practice strongly encouraged by his mother, to whom he was very close. His other interest was poetry, particularly the works of Shelley and Keats. He began writing poetry of his own, though he was not encouraged in this by his father, Thomas, who advised his son to seek more stable employment.

After failing to secure a scholarship to the University of London, Owen spent some time assisting a vicar in Oxfordshire, providing social care to the local community in order to gauge his suitability for a career as a clergyman. He abandoned this ambition in 1913, after growing disillusioned with how ineffective the church was in helping the poor, and travelled to France to teach at the Berlitz Language School in Bordeaux. He remained there the following year as the fog of war descended. During that time, Owen's poetic sensibility was greatly influenced by the French poet Laurent Tailhade, with whom he developed a close friendship.

Owen returned to England in October 1915 and enlisted. He was commissioned as a second lieutenant in the Manchester Regiment the following year. Early in 1917, he joined the 2nd Battalion, which had been decimated in the 140-day Battle of the Somme the year before. With them, he experienced first hand the horrors of trench warfare. Up to this point, most of his literary energy had been invested in writing letters to his mother. But the freezing temperatures, incessant gunfire and the ever-present fear of poison-gas and death stirred his poetic genius. In March, he fell 15 feet through a shell-hole and into a cellar where he lay for three days. A few weeks later, he was blown into the air by an artillery shell in a trench near St Quentin, diagnosed with neurasthenia (shell-shock) and sent back to England.

He was admitted to Craiglockhart War Hospital, near Edinburgh, under the care of Dr Arthur Brock. Dr Brock's theory was that victims of this condition had to confront the horrors of their experiences in order to come to terms with them. The treatment had a miraculous effect on Owen, whose reaction was an astonishing outpouring of creative energy. He was further inspired when another poet, Siegfried Sassoon, arrived at Craiglockhart for treatment. Though their relationship was brief, it burned brightly, with Sassoon offering support, advice and encouragement to his new friend. Within weeks, Owen had recovered and he wrote feverishly, using his first-hand experiences to warn his readers of what he called 'the pity of war'.

Owen left the hospital in October 1917. His words continued to flow during the next few months as he rubbed shoulders with writers and other literary figures. He also began compiling a collection of his work for the publisher William Heinemann.

Despite his anti-war stance, Owen was keen to return to the front and was declared fit for active duty in August 1918. In October, he was awarded the Military Cross for 'conspicuous gallantry' in capturing a German machine-gun. He was killed a month later, on 4 November 1918, one week before the war's end. His mother received the news on Armistice Day, as the local church bells rang out in celebration.

Lines Written on My Nineteenth Birthday

March 18, 1912

Two Spirits woke me from my sleep this morn;
Both most unwelcome were; for they have torn
Away from me the shady screens of ease
And unreflecting, unself-scanning Peace
Wherein I used to hide me from annoy
In years which found and left me still a Boy.
The First rose solemn, with a Voice of stern
Monition; and it said: 'Look back! and learn
To number life by moments, not by years;
Know that thy youth to its completion nears.
This night the final minute hath been laid
Upon thy nineteen Springs. Aye, be dismayed
To see the Fourth Part of thy utmost Span
Now spent! What then? Affrighted dost thou plan
To crowd the Rest with Action, every whit?
Ev'n so essay; but know thou canst not knit
Thy web of hours so close as to regain
E'en one lost stitch! For ever gaps remain!'
Hereat it ceased; for now a second Shade
Caught all my senses to't; no sound it made;
No form it had; but quietly it drew
Its tightening hand of Pain through every thew
Of my frail body.... Pain? – Why Pain today?
Sure, not a taste of what this tingling clay
Shall suffer through the year? And yet, if so,
'Twill be but my most rightful share, I trow,
Scarce worse than the keen hunger-pinch that racks
Numberless wretches all their life. Pain slacks

Its hold on one, only to grasp another;
And why should I be spared, and not my brother?

So thinking, quickly I pass the day. And lo!
What kindnesses the Friends around me show!
How many eyes in warm solicitude
Have smiled upon me! Tongues that have been rude
Are gentle now.... Yet still, how do I miss
Thine eyes, *thy* voice, my Mother! Oft I kiss
Thy portrait, and I clutch thy letter dear
As if it were thy hand.

At this, fresh cheer
Comes over me; and now upon my couch
Of ruby velvet, o'er the fire I crouch
In full content. I only pause from reading
To scribble these few lines; or, scarcely heeding
The dismal damp abroad, to mock the rain
Shooting its sleety balls at me in vain.
– Ho, thus, methinks, hereafter, when the weak
Creations of a Mental Mist shall seek
To quench my soul, I'll thwart them by the shield
Of crystal Hope!
For there have been revealed
Heart-secrets since the coming of this day,
Making me thankful for its thorn-paved way.
Among them this: 'No joy is comparable
Unto the *Melting* – soft and gradual –
Of Torture's needles in the flesh. To sail
Smoothly from out the abysmal anguish-jail
And tread the placid plains of *normal ease*
Is sweeter far, I deem, than all the glees

Which we may catch by mounting higher still
Into the dangerous air where actual Bliss doth thrill.'

A Rhymed Epistle to E.L.G.

'Heigh ho! Howe dothe old Tyme gallop.'
Bacon, *Promus*

1

My honoured cousin,
I'll not dwell
Longtime upon your verse (so well
Conceived) yet I am bound to tell
How after many a patient puff,
And later, many an angry snuff,
I got into a regular huff
That you had never written
To say how badly bitten
You were by your exam,
Or else how well you'd smitten
The Oxford-Senior Witan
By letting off your cram.
However…;
So clever,
So well selected,
And so unexpected
Was this your happy rime
It makes amend
For lapse of time,
So here I end,
My chiding chime.

2

… 'Is it physical To walk unbraced, and suck up the
humours Of the dank morning?'
Cool-as a Cheeser, Bacon
I will no more than mention
The Keswick grand convention
Such speech would be amiss
In such a thing as this.
What I can best remember
Of Keswick was the Camp
Pitched in a field as damp
As gutters in December.
We woke at six or thereabouts;
We woke to find our inner clouts
As moist as Caustic Soda;
To find our tent, a bell-tent,
A very bell-jar, feculent
With CO2, Cl, strong-blent
With every pungent odour.
We lay at night between wet rugs
Found nothing, though, that rhymed with rugs –
And were the rugs a bit less hairy,
And were the tent a bit more airy,
Had fewer been the chilly gouts
That dropped upon our snoring snouts,
And warmer been the morning blast,
And daintier been the plain repast,
Less like strong bilge the stuff called tea,
Less like roast wood the pie-pastry
More plentiful the fruit and berry

3

'Hail!' Bacon's Midsummer Iced Cream Act III, scene i
I went to Coniston one day
And twice got drenched and had to pay
Hotels to dry the wet away.
The hail hailed, pricked and pained;
The rain rained, rained, and rained;
The clouds clouded, crowded round;
The thunder thundered; the wind – wound.

4

1 'Awake.' Isaiah.
2 'Come forth.' Bacon, King John, Act IV, sc. i.
3 'Come, prepare yourself' do.
4 'See'st thou you littel birde?' Chaucer.
5 'Thank you.' Christopher Marlowe.

All such as dwelled in the tent of Sh! Hem!
Now none of that! I mean – all them
As cohabit my canvas limpet
Were photographed thereby; and some imp hit
On th' idea of appearing in nightclo'es
(As the photographer came before 8 a.m.)
So in turbans of towels, and baggy pyjamas
We were actually taken; and what with the right-pose,
Right-exposure, et cetera, we look like real 'salaamers'.

5

'Damn all thieves'
Keats
I can see how you stare
At this startling quotation,

Quite amazed that I dare
Say that Keats thus could swear.
But 'tis a citation
From one of his letters,
And I make no filtration
Of words of my betters;
So there!
And indeed I would add
'Secret Borrowers too',
And every vile cad
To whose mind 'me and you'
Are one and the same.
For I think it a shame
That my bike, so well prized,
Some knaves have bestridden,
And one has so ridden
As to hug a stone wall
Or somehow to fall,
And has made a nice mess,
(Shape of pedal – an S)
Hurt the mudguard no less
And the nickel and all!

Epilogue

'Wind up' Bacon, King Lear, Act IV, sc, vii
I tried in an hour
To concoct this epistle;
– 'Twas beyond my poor power,
And, by that deep Whistle,
I've been nearly two.
Time, then, for dismissal

And closing adieu.
Dear fellow, do send me
Another of yours
For I've none to befriend me
When Dunsden immures.
And perhaps I will send you
Another of mine.
And so I commend you
To heaven benign.

Sweet Is Your Antique Body

Sweet is your antique body, not yet young;
Beauty withheld from youth that looks for youth;
Fair only for your father. Dear among
Masters in art. To all men else uncouth;
Save me, who know your smile comes very old,
Learnt of the happy dead that laughed with gods;
For earlier suns than ours have lent you gold;
Sly fauns and trees have given you jigs and nods.

But soon your heart, hot-beating like a bird's,
Shall slow down. Youth shall lop your hair;
And you must learn wry meanings in our words.
Your smile shall dull, because too keen aware;
And when for hopes your hand shall be uncurled,
Your eyes shall close, being open to the world.

Autumnal

If it be very strange and sorrowful
To scent the first night-frost in autumntide;
If on the moaning eve when Summer died
Men shuddered, awed to hear her burial;
And if the dissolution of one rose
(Whereof the future holds unnumbered store)
Engender human tears, – ah! how much more
Sorrows and suffers be whose sense foreknows
The weakening and the withering of a love,
The dying of a love that had been dear!
Who feels upon a hand, but late love-warm,
A hardness of indifference, like a glove;
And in the dead calm of a voice may hear
The menace of a drear and mighty storm.

Science Has Looked

Science has looked, and sees no life but this:
Or, at the most 'tis hypothetical.
'Thou art as animals, as worms, as clay;
Earth – thy small planet, of a thousand, one –
Shall slowly waste, unto an outburnt ash:
And thou and all thy race, be blotted out.
For in the dissolution of man's brain
Himself dissolves, and passes into naught'…

O careful Science, thou had'st all my zeal,
But a Third Power smiles, and beckons me.
She is a wanton of too light a name
To hold the faith of most men in her heart.
Poor Poesy! She hath no constancy…

But yesterday she clung half-trustingly
To calm religion. Where is she today?
Clasping Cold Science with a grim embrace!
No constancy! But comforts manifold,
And therefore, lovely to a waif, like me!

Speak to me Poesy! Give me on this height
The one true message of thy thousand oracles!

'Yea? Cryest thou so hungry for some Light?
Seek light no more! There is no Light as yet!
The Light that lights the soul shall be the last
Created thing; as that which lights the eye the first!
These mountains are the breasts of Mother Earth,

Nestle thou there, child; suck thy fill of joys.
And strive no more to look beyond thy Mother's arms.'

– So? Is it so? Then I will lie and rest.
O – mountains, there comes over me this hour
A wondrous longing for my latest sleep.
I long to drowse, and fall upon eternal sleep;
I want to sleep, but not to dream, and not to wake;
Pass hence, and yet behold no region more;
Fade from this company of distracted men
Where all mad deluders, or else sick deluded…

Now, Night, rise softly like a careful nurse:
Lower the lights of day round thy sick child:
For I would sleep…
Poor I, who know not what I am, nor whence,
Would shake away this bitter case of flesh,
Even though naught remain when it is gone.
Would rid me of long deceiving blood;
How know I but at this very hour
My thoughts most high, most melancholy-grand,
Be not the chance-distemper of my pulse,
The doing of some small, intestine flaw!
O death, before I pluck my brain away,
Let me but sleep…
        My heart stops – it is well…
O Light, which art but darkness,
O cruel world… O Men… O my own Self…
Farewell!

Written in a Wood, September 1910

Full ninety autumns hath this ancient beech
Helped with its myriad leafy tongues to swell
The dirges of the deep-toned western gale,
And ninety times hath all its power of speech
Been stricken dumb, at sound of winter's yell,
Since Adonais, no more strong and hale,
Might have rejoiced to linger here and teach
His thoughts in sonnets to the listening dell;
Or glide in fancy through those leafy grots
And bird-pavilions hung with arras green,
To hear the sonnets of its minstrel choir.
Ah, ninety times again, when autumn rots
Shall birds and leaves be mute and all unseen,
Yet shall I see fair Keats, and hear his lyre.

Sonnet, Written at Teignmouth, on a Pilgrimage to Keats's House

Three colours have I known the Deep to wear;
'Tis well today that Purple grandeurs gloom,
Veiling the Emerald sheen and Sky-blue glare.
Well, too, that lowly-brooding clouds now loom
In sable majesty around, fringed fair
With ermine-white of surf: to me they bear
Watery memorials of His mystic doom
Whose Name was writ in Water (saith his tomb).

Eternally may sad waves wail his death,
Choke in their grief 'mongst rocks where he has lain,
Or heave in silence, yearning with hushed breath,
While mournfully trail the slow-moved mists and rain,
And softly the small drops slide from weeping trees,
Quivering in anguish to the sobbing breeze.

To Eros

In that I loved you, Love, I worshipped you;
In that I worshipped well, I sacrificed.
All of most worth I bound and burnt and slew:
The innocent small things, fair friends and Christ.

I slew all falser loves, I slew all true,
For truth is the prime lie men tell a boy.
Glory I cast away, as bridegrooms do
Their splendid garments in their haste of joy.

But when I fell and held your sandalled feet,
You laughed; you loosed away my lips; you rose.
I heard the singing of your wings' retreat;
And watched you, far-flown, flush the Olympian snows,
Beyond my hoping. Starkly I returned
To stare upon the ash of all I burned.

The Promisers

When I awoke, the glancing day looked gay;
The air said: Fare you fleetly; you will meet him!
And when the prosp'rous sun was well begun,
I heard a bird say: Sweetly you shall greet him!

The sun fell strong and bold upon my shoulder;
It hung, it clung as it were my friend's arm.
The birds fifed on before, shrill-piping pipers,
Right down to town; and there they ceased to charm.

And there I wandered till the noon came soon,
And chimed: The time is hastening with his face!
Sly twilight said: I bring him; wait till late!
But darkness harked forlorn to my lone pace.

The Rime of the Youthful Mariner

One knotted a rope with an evil knout,
    And flogged me till I fell;
And he is picking the rope end out
    In a land-locked prison-cell.

One tied my wrist with a twisted cord
    While I lay asleep on deck.
But his reward was overboard,
    With the string around his neck.

One bound my mouth with her hands of silk,
    And drew me backward so.
Her skin that was foul as curdled milk
    Is fouler today, I trow.

One clogged my feet with a heavy wine,
    And my tongue with a tangling drug.
But now his tongue is thicker than mine
    And black as any slug.

One bound my thighs with his muscled arm,
    Whose weight was good to bear.
O may he come to no worse harm
    Than what he wrought me there.

Impromptu

Now, let me feel the feeling of thy hand –
For it is softer than the breasts of girls,
And warmer than the pillows of their cheeks,
And richer than the fullness of their eyes,
And stronger than the ardour of their hearts.

Its shape is subtler than a dancer's limbs;
Its skin is coloured like the twilight Alp;
And odoured like the pale, night-scented flowers,
And fresh with early love, as earth with dawn.

Yield me thy hand a little while, fair love;
That I may feel it; and so feel thy life,
And kiss across it, as the sea the sand,
And love it, with the love of Sun for Earth.

Ah! let me look a long while in thine eyes,
For they are deeper than the depths of thought,
And clearer than the ether after rain,
And suaver than the moving of the moon,
And vaster than the void of all desire.

Child, let me fully see and know those eyes!
Their fire is like the wrath of shaken rubies;
Their shade is like the peaceful forest-heart.

They hold me as the great star holds the less.
I see them as the lights beyond this life.
They reach me by a sense not found in man,
And bless me with a bliss unguessed of God.

A Palinode

Some little while ago, I had a mood
When what we know as 'Nature' seemed to me
So sympathetic, ample, sweet, and good
That I preferred it to Society.

Not for a season, be it understood,
But altogether and perpetually.
As far as feeling went, I thought I could
Be quit of men, live independently.

For men and minds, heart-humours and heart's-tease
Disturbed without exciting: whereas woods,
The seasonal changes, and the chanting seas
Were both soul-rousing and sense-lulling. Moods,

Such moods prolonged, became a mania.
I found the stark stretch of a bleak-blown moor
Least barren of all places. Mere extranea
Seemed populace and town: things to ignore.

But if the sovereign sun I might behold
With condescension coming down benign,
And blessing all the field and air with gold,
Then the contentment of the world was mine.

In secret deserts where the night was nude
And each excited star grew ardent-eyed,
I tasted more than this life's plenitude,
And far as farthest stars perceive, I spied.

Once, when the whiteness of the spectral moon
Had terrorized the creatures of the wold,
When that long staring of the glazed-eyed
Had stupefied the land and made it cold,

I fell seduced into a madness; for,
Forgetting in that night the life of days,
I said I had no need of fellows more,
I madly hated men and all their ways.

I hated, feeling hated; I supposed
That others did not need me any more.
The book of human knowledge I then closed;
Passion, art, science? Trifles to ignore.

But in my error, men ignored not me,
And did not let me in my moonbeams bask.
And I took antidotes; though what they be
Unless yourself be poisoned, do not ask.

For I am overdosed. The City now
Holds all my passion; these my soul most feels:
Crowds surging; racket of traffic; market row;
Bridges, sonorous under rapid wheels;

Pacific lamentations of a bell;
The smoking of the old men at their doors;
All attitudes of children; the farewell
And casting-off of ships for far-off shores.

The Rivals

If thou guessed what easy hours
I can fleet among my flowers,
How I fondle them, and how
Find them better friends than Thou,
Haply, love, the thing might shame thee;
Haply with some spite inflame thee.
Nay, indeed, thou art not all;
And I can forget thy thrall.
For I shall when summer comes
Sport me with my garden chums,
Orchid, harebell, fern, and foxglove.
Then thou'lt tear thy pretty locks, love,
Twisting curls round jealous fingers...;
When thou find'st thy true love lingers
Longer o'er the rose than thee,
Know thou hast great rivalry;
Cry to see it, careless elf,
Bite thy lips, but blame thyself!
Many a slim tree, dark of tresses,
Whispering, gives me strange caresses.
Steadfast shines Narcissus' eye
When I would his beauty try.
And he loads my sighs with scent,
Not with frowns of discontent.
Water lilies all tranquil lie
When their secrecies I spy.
Ruddy pout the mouths of roses –
More I kiss, more each uncloses.
Even violets, who are shy
Of their cousin in the sky,

Do not stiffen or resent
When a fingertip is bent
Round their chins. And if, like thee,
Little snowdrops were foot-free,
Would they run from me, and vent
Laughs of scornful merriment?
Nay, they love me, as I them.
Oh, my loves of bud and stem,
Tell my Maid what lightsome hours
I spend with you in your bowers
This may pique her jealousy;
Haply charm her back to me.

O Believe that God Gives You All that He Promises

O – believe that God gives you
All that he promises
A Saviour who forgives you,
A perfect Saviour,
A Saviour full of power
On the earth and in the heavens,
A Saviour whose presence
Alone makes happy.
This Saviour will make you live
As he has lived.
You will be able to follow him everywhere
Without being conquered.
Right to the end, in the conflict,
His arm will protect you
And in the dark valley
He will lead you.

The Sleeping Beauty

Sojourning through a southern realm in youth,
I came upon a house by happy chance
Where bode a marvellous Beauty. There, romance
Flew faerily until I lit on truth –
For lo! the fair Child slumbered. Though, forsooth,
She lay not blanketed in drowsy trance,
But leapt alert of limb and keen of glance,
From sun to shower; from gaiety to ruth;
Yet breathed her loveliness asleep in her:
For, when I kissed, her eyelids knew no stir.
So back I drew tiptoe from that Princess,
Because it was too soon, and not my part,
To start voluptuous pulses in her heart,
And kiss her to the world of Consciousness.

Schoolmistress

Having, with bold Horatius, stamped her feet
And waved a final swashing arabesque
O'er the brave days of old, she ceased to bleat,
Slapped her Macaulay back upon the desk,
Resumed her calm gaze and her lofty seat.

There, while she heard the classic lines repeat,
Once more the teacher's face clenched stern;
For through the window, looking on the street,
Three soldiers hailed her. She made no return.
One was called 'Orace whom she would not greet.

From My Diary, July 1914

Leaves
    Murmuring by myriads in the shimmering trees.
Lives
    Wakening with wonder in the Pyrenees.
Birds
    Cheerily chirping in the early day.
Bards
    Singing of summer, scything through the hay.
Bees
    Shaking the heavy dews from bloom and frond.
Boys
    Bursting the surface of the ebony pond.
Flashes
    Of swimmers carving through the sparkling cold.
Fleshes
    Gleaming with wetness to the morning gold.
A mead
    Bordered about with warbling waterbrooks.
A maid
    Laughing the love-laugh with me; proud of looks.
The heat
    Throbbing between the upland and the peak.
Her heart
    Quivering with passion to my pr'ssed cheek.
Braiding
    Of floating flames across the mountain brow.
Brooding
    Of stillness; and a sighing of the bough.

Stirs
    Of leaflets in the gloom; soft petal-showers;
Stars
    Expanding with the starr'd nocturnal flowers.

A Little Health, A Little Wealth

A Little Health, A Little Wealth, A Little
House, and Freedom – and at The End,
I'd Like a Friend, And Every Cause to Need Him.

Miners

There was a whispering in my hearth,
        A sigh of the coal.
Grown wistful of a former earth
        It might recall.

I listened for a tale of leaves
        And smothered ferns,
Frond-forests; and the low, sly lives
        Before the fawns.

My fire might show steam-phantoms simmer
        From Time's old cauldron,
Before the birds made nests in summer,
        Or men had children.

But the coals were murmuring of their mine,
        And moans down there
Of boys that slept wry sleep, and men
        Writhing for air.

And I saw white bones in the cinder-shard,
        Bones without number.
For many hearts with coal are charred,
        And few remember.

I thought of all that worked dark pits
        Of war, and died
Digging the rock where Death reputes
        Peace lies indeed.

Comforted years will sit soft-chaired
In rooms of amber;
The years will stretch their hands, well-cheered
By our life's ember.

The centuries will burn rich loads
With which we groaned,
Whose warmth shall lull their dreaming lids,
While songs are crooned.
But they will not dream of us poor lads
Left in the ground.

Roundel

In Shrewsbury Town e'en Hercules wox tired,
Tired of the streets that end not up nor down;
Tired of the Quarry, though seats may be hired
Of Shrewsbury Town.

Tired of the tongues that knew not his renown;
Tired of the Quarry Bye-Laws, so admired
By the Salopian, the somnambulant clown.

Weak as a babe, and in like wise attired,
He leaned upon his club; frowned a last frown,
And of ineffable boredom, so expired
In Shrewsbury Town.

1914

War broke: and now the Winter of the world
With perishing great darkness closes in.
The foul tornado, centred at Berlin,
Is over all the width of Europe whirled,
Rending the sails of progress. Rent or furled
Are all Art's ensigns. Verse wails. Now begin
Famines of thought and feeling. Love's wine's thin.
The grain of human Autumn rots, down-hurled.

For after Spring had bloomed in early Greece,
And Summer blazed her glory out with Rome,
An Autumn softly fell, a harvest home,
A slow grand age, and rich with all increase.
But now, for us, wild Winter, and the need
Of sowings for new Spring, and blood for seed.

Arms and the Boy

Let the boy try along this bayonet-blade
How cold steel is, and keen with hunger of blood;
Blue with all malice, like a madman's flash;
And thinly drawn with famishing for flesh.

Lend him to stroke these blind, blunt bullet-leads,
Which long to nuzzle in the hearts of lads,
Or give him cartridges of fine zinc teeth
Sharp with the sharpness of grief and death.

For his teeth seem for laughing round an apple.
There lurk no claws behind his fingers supple;
And God will grow no talons at his heels,
Nor antlers through the thickness of his curls.

Ballad of Kings and Christs

1

The Women
When blood must pay the reckoning,
Lest heart go unsufficed;
When bodies are the offering
Lest souls be sacrificed;

Let everyman live Arthur King,
And any man die Christ.

2

No underling pays reckoning
For Britain princely priced;
No hireling is the offering
So freely sacrificed.

But everyman was Arthur King
Who died the death of Christ.

3

The Slain
Verily so are we become,
Who we're rough lads before?
The Women
Holy ye passed from home; from home
And sunshine evermore.

And Arthur ran with everyman
That crossed the hell to Christ.

4

The Slain

Is the sun sweet, on rose, on wheat?
Do little lads sing cheery?
Quiet the street, for cripples' feet,
And gardens for the weary?

In everything is Arthur King
If many a man die Christ?

5

The Women

Yea, days of gold await the old,
The childrens' cheeks are ruddy;
Because ye bold, ye Christs, grow old,
And your dear cheeks are bloody,

But while blood sings ye are our Kings
And Christs till prayers are told.

6

The Slain

The soil is safe … for widow and waif?

Women

And for the soul of Britain,
Because marred bodies ye vouchsafe,
To save the soul unsmitten.

The Slain

Shall he return, Lord Arthur stern,
To keep the land for Christ?

7

The Women

They are returned for whom we yearned,
Both Arthur and the Christ;
And souls have learned, our hearts discerned:
Ye were the King, the Christ!

We heard the shout, we saw the rout,
We knew the Kings' return.

8

For lo! Each man stood Arthur's span
Who stood the Saxon flood,
And every lad was seraph – clad
Who wore his own bright blood:

Hail to the earth in second birth!
Hail, Arthur! Hail, Lord Christ!

Dulce et Decorum Est

Bent double, like old beggars under sacks,
Knock-kneed, coughing like hags, we cursed through
sludge,
Till on the haunting flares we turned our backs,
And towards our distant rest began to trudge.
Men marched asleep. Many had lost their boots,
But limped on, blood-shod. All went lame; all
blind;
Drunk with fatigue; deaf even to the hoots
Of gas-shells dropping softly behind.

Gas! GAS! Quick, boys! – An ecstasy of fumbling
Fitting the clumsy helmets just in time,
But someone still was yelling out and stumbling
And flound'ring like a man in fire or lime...
Dim through the misty panes and thick green
light,
As under a green sea, I saw him drowning.

In all my dreams before my helpless sight,
He plunges at me, guttering, choking, drowning.

If in some smothering dreams, you too could pace
Behind the wagon that we flung him in,
And watch the white eyes writhing in his face,
His hanging face, like a devil's sick of sin;
If you could hear, at every jolt, the blood
Come gargling from the froth-corrupted lungs,
Obscene as cancer, bitter as the cud
Of vile, incurable sores on innocent tongues, –

My friend, you would not tell with such high zest
To children ardent for some desperate glory,
The old Lie: *Dulce et decorum est*
Pro patria mori.

Disabled

He sat in a wheeled chair, waiting for dark,
And shivered in his ghastly suit of grey,
Legless, sewn short at elbow. Through the park
Voices of boys rang saddening like a hymn,
Voices of play and pleasure after day,
Till gathering sleep had mothered them from him.

* * *

About this time Town used to swing so gay
When glow-lamps budded in the light-blue trees,
And girls glanced lovelier as the air grew dim, –
In the old times, before he threw away his knees.
Now he will never feel again how slim
Girls' waists are, or how warm their subtle hands,
All of them touch him like some queer disease.

* * *

There was an artist silly for his face,
For it was younger than his youth, last year.
Now, he is old; his back will never brace;
He's lost his colour very far from here,
Poured it down shell-holes till the veins ran dry,
And half his lifetime lapsed in the hot race
And leap of purple spurted from his thigh.

* * *

One time he liked a blood-smear down his leg,
After the matches carried shoulder-high.
It was after football, when he'd drunk a peg,
He thought he'd better join. He wonders why.
Someone had said he'd look a god in kilts.
That's why; and maybe, too, to please his Meg,
Aye, that was it, to please the giddy jilts,
He asked to join. He didn't have to beg;
Smiling they wrote his lie: aged nineteen years.
Germans he scarcely thought of, all their guilt,
And Austria's, did not move him. And no fears
Of Fear came yet. He thought of jewelled hilts
For daggers in plaid socks; of smart salutes;
And care of arms; and leave; and pay arrears;
Esprit de corps; and hints for young recruits.
And soon, he was drafted out with drums and cheers.

* * *

Some cheered him home, but not as crowds cheer Goal.
Only a solemn man who brought him fruits
Thanked him; and then enquired about his soul.

* * *

Now, he will spend a few sick years in institutes,
And do what things the rules consider wise,
And take whatever pity they may dole.
Tonight he noticed how the women's eyes
Passed from him to the strong men that were whole.
How cold and late it is! Why don't they come
And put him into bed? Why don't they come?

Sonnet (Whither is Passed the Softly-Vanished Day)

Whither is passed the softly-vanished day?
It is not lost: though seeming gone for aye;
For as no bar of incense fumeth out,
But leaveth softer perfume all about,
So hours pleasant, though they must waste away,
Through memory's holy cells like odours stray;
And steal on us, as entering there devout,
We close the door against the world without.

Nor days alone are thus conserved and freed,
Sweet lives, by their consuming, sweeter grow,
And larger and more wholly soul, released.
Prayers not the incense which the high gods heed,
But the spent essence from a life aglow,
Perfumeth heaven with fragrance unsurceased.

Exposure

Our brains ache, in the merciless iced east winds that
knive us…
Wearied we keep awake because the night is silent…
Low drooping flares confuse our memory of the salient…
Worried by silence, sentries whisper, curious, nervous,
But nothing happens.

Watching, we hear the mad gusts tugging on the wire,
Like twitching agonies of men among its brambles.
Northward, incessantly, the flickering gunnery rumbles,
Far off, like a dull rumour of some other war.
What are we doing here?

The poignant misery of dawn begins to grow…
We only know war lasts, rain soaks, and clouds sag
stormy.
Dawn massing in the east her melancholy army
Attacks once more in ranks on shivering ranks of grey,
But nothing happens.

Sudden successive flights of bullets streak the silence.
Less deadly than the air that shudders black with snow,
With sidelong flowing flakes that flock, pause, and renew,
We watch them wandering up and down the wind's
nonchalance,
But nothing happens.

Pale flakes with fingering stealth come feeling for our
faces –

We cringe in holes, back on forgotten dreams, and stare,
snow-dazed,
Deep into grassier ditches. So we drowse, sun-dozed,
Littered with blossoms trickling where the blackbird
fusses.
– Is it that we are dying?

Slowly our ghosts drag home: glimpsing the sunk fires,
glozed
With crusted dark-red jewels; crickets jingle there;
For hours the innocent mice rejoice: the house is theirs;
Shutters and doors, all closed: on us the doors are
closed, –
We turn back to our dying.

Since we believe not otherwise can kind fires burn;
Now ever suns smile true on child, or field, or fruit.
For God's invincible spring our love is made afraid;
Therefore, not loath, we lie out here; therefore were born,
For love of God seems dying.

Tonight, this frost will fasten on this mud and us,
Shrivelling many hands, and puckering foreheads crisp.
The burying-party, picks and shovels in shaking grasp,
Pause over half-known faces. All their eyes are ice,
But nothing happens.

Futility

Move him into the sun –
Gently its touch awoke him once,
At home, whispering of fields half-sown.
Always it woke him, even in France,
Until this morning and this snow.
If anything might rouse him now
The kind old sun will know.

Think how it wakes the seeds –
Woke once the clays of a cold star.
Are limbs, so dear-achieved, are sides
Full-nerved, still warm, too hard to stir?
Was it for this the clay grew tall?
– O what made fatuous sunbeams toil
To break earth's sleep at all?

Insensibility

1

Happy are men who yet before they are killed
Can let their veins run cold.
Whom no compassion fleers
Or makes their feet
Sore on the alleys cobbled with their brothers.
The front line withers.
But they are troops who fade, not flowers,
For poets' tearful fooling:
Men, gaps for filling:
Losses, who might have fought
Longer; but no one bothers.

2

And some cease feeling
Even themselves or for themselves.
Dullness best solves
The tease and doubt of shelling,
And Chance's strange arithmetic
Comes simpler than the reckoning of their shilling.
They keep no check on armies' decimation.

3

Happy are these who lose imagination:
They have enough to carry with ammunition.
Their spirit drags no pack.
Their old wounds, save with cold, can not more ache.
Having seen all things red,
Their eyes are rid
Of the hurt of the colour of blood for ever.

And terror's first constriction over,
Their hearts remain small-drawn.
Their senses in some scorching cautery of battle
Now long since ironed,
Can laugh among the dying, unconcerned.

4

Happy the soldier home, with not a notion
How somewhere, every dawn, some men attack,
And many sighs are drained.
Happy the lad whose mind was never trained:
His days are worth forgetting more than not.
He sings along the march
Which we march taciturn, because of dusk,
The long, forlorn, relentless trend
From larger day to huger night.

5

We wise, who with a thought besmirch
Blood over all our soul,
How should we see our task
But through his blunt and lashless eyes?
Alive, he is not vital overmuch;
Dying, not mortal overmuch;
Nor sad, nor proud,
Nor curious at all.
He cannot tell
Old men's placidity from his.

6

But cursed are dullards whom no cannon stuns,
That they should be as stones.

Wretched are they, and mean
With paucity that never was simplicity.
By choice they made themselves immune
To pity and whatever moans in man
Before the last sea and the hapless stars;
Whatever mourns when many leave these shores;
Whatever shares
The eternal reciprocity of tears.

Anthem for Doomed Youth

What passing-bells for these who die as cattle?
    – Only the monstrous anger of the guns.
    Only the stuttering rifles' rapid rattle
Can patter out their hasty orisons.
No mockeries now for them; no prayers nor bells;
    Nor any voice of mourning save the choirs, –
The shrill, demented choirs of wailing shells;
    And bugles calling for them from sad shires.

What candles may be held to speed them all?
    Not in the hands of boys, but in their eyes
Shall shine the holy glimmers of goodbyes.
    The pallor of girls' brows shall be their pall;
Their flowers the tenderness of patient minds,
And each slow dusk a drawing-down of blinds.

The Last Laugh

'O Jesus Christ! I'm hit,' he said; and died.
Whether he vainly cursed or prayed indeed,
        The Bullets chirped – In vain, vain, vain!
        Machine-guns chuckled – Tut-tut! Tut-tut!
        And the Big Gun guffawed.

Another sighed, – 'O Mother, – mother, – Dad!'
Then smiled at nothing, childlike, being dead.
        And the lofty Shrapnel-cloud
        Leisurely gestured, – Fool!
        And the splinters spat, and tittered.

'My Love!' one moaned. Love-languid seemed his mood,
Till slowly lowered, his whole face kissed the mud.
        And the Bayonets' long teeth grinned;
        Rabbles of Shells hooted and groaned;
        And the Gas hissed.

S.I.W.

I will to the King,
And offer him consolation in his trouble,
For that man there has set his teeth to die,
And being one that hates obedience,
Discipline, and orderliness of life,
I cannot mourn him.
W.B. YEATS

I. The Prologue

Patting good-bye, doubtless they told the lad
He'd always show the Hun a brave man's face;
Father would sooner him dead than in disgrace, –
Was proud to see him going, aye, and glad.
Perhaps his mother whimpered how she'd fret
Until he got a nice safe wound to nurse.
Sisters would wish girls too could shoot, charge, curse …
Brothers – would send his favourite cigarette.
Each week, month after month, they wrote the same,
Thinking him sheltered in some Y.M. Hut,
Because he said so, writing on his butt
Where once an hour a bullet missed its aim
And misses teased the hunger of his brain.
His eyes grew old with wincing, and his hand
Reckless with ague. Courage leaked, as sand
From the best sand-bags after years of rain.
But never leave, wound, fever, trench-foot, shock,
Untrapped the wretch. And death seemed still withheld
For torture of lying machinally shelled,
At the pleasure of this world's Powers who'd run amok.

He'd seen men shoot their hands, on night patrol.
Their people never knew. Yet they were vile.
'Death sooner than dishonour, that's the style!'
So Father said.

II. The Action

One dawn, our wire patrol
Carried him. This time, Death had not missed.
We could do nothing but wipe his bleeding cough.
Could it be accident? – Rifles go off…
Not sniped? No. (Later they found the English ball.)

III. The Poem

It was the reasoned crisis of his soul
Against more days of inescapable thrall,
Against infrangibly wired and blind trench wall
Curtained with fire, roofed in with creeping fire,
Slow grazing fire, that would not burn him whole
But kept him for death's promises and scoff,
And life's half-promising, and both their riling.

IV. The Epilogue

With him they buried the muzzle his teeth had kissed,
And truthfully wrote the Mother, 'Tim died smiling.'

The Send-Off

Down the close, darkening lanes they sang their way
To the siding-shed,
And lined the train with faces grimly gay.

Their breasts were stuck all white with wreath and spray
As men's are, dead.

Dull porters watched them, and a casual tramp
Stood staring hard,
Sorry to miss them from the upland camp.

Then, unmoved, signals nodded, and a lamp
Winked to the guard.

So secretly, like wrongs hushed-up, they went.
They were not ours:
We never heard to which front these were sent.

Nor there if they yet mock what women meant
Who gave them flowers.

Shall they return to beatings of great bells
In wild train-loads?
A few, a few, too few for drums and yells,

May creep back, silent, to village wells,
Up half-known roads.

The Little Mermaid

Of Hans Christian Anderson

Part I

1

Far out at sea, the water is as blue
As cornflowers, and as clear as crystal-core;
But so exceeding deep, no sea-bird's view
Can fathom it, nor men's ropes touch its floor.
Strange, snake-like trees and weeds – the same which grew
Before dry land with herbs was peopled o'er –
Still sleep in heavy peacefulness down there,
And hold their fluctuous arms towards upper air.

2

And it is there the Sea-King's nation dwells.
His palace, golden-bright and ruby-red,
Gleams like a crown among those velvet dells.
Pink, shimmering streams of light its windows shed,
Like waterfalls of wine; and pink-white shells,
Like Alpine snows, its lofty roof o'erspread;
Which close and open, close and open wide,
With every ebb and flowing of the tide.

3

Twice beauteous is the sight, for perfect pearls
Glimmer between the valvelets as they gape.
As when a butterfly shut wings unfurls,
And pollen-filmed globes of dew escape,
So ope those shells, so shine those gems. The swirls

Of stirring currents stroke to smoothest shape
The sandy palace floors; or, like a breeze,
Suddenly fluster its mysterious trees.

4

The ancient King, of consort long bereft,
Unto his mother gave the queenly state;
And in her careful governance he left
His six fair daughters. Scarce could I relate
The beauty of those six without a theft
Of honey-words from some song-potentate;
And of the youngest's utter loveliness,
I rest content to wake a wistful guess.

5

Her skin is delicate and freshly clear
As petals of wild rose; and in her eyes,
As in the stillness of an evening mere,
All heaven's purple concentrated lies.
But lo! what marvel to mankind is here:
She has no feet, no knees! but mermaid-wise,
A fish's tail, smooth-tapering from her waist,
Blue-scaled, and glistering, like silver chased.

6

All day, these mermaids sported in their hall,
Feeding the fish that through the windows shot,
And training weeds to twine about the wall.
Or sometimes each would tend her garden grot,
Where one so ranged her plants as to recall
Blunt-snouted whales; another planned her plot

In shapes to imitate her own; and one,
The youngest, choosing red flowers, made a sun.

7

A strange and lonely child seemed this Princess.
Deep were the fathomings of her secret thought.
Not that she shunned a sisterly caress;
But, spoken to, faint-smiled, and answered naught.
Loved she the silent deep? Nay, less and less
She loved it! And as years new sameness brought,
Its silence, its low stillness, its pale gloom,
Weighed on her soul, and made sweet life a doom.

8

Her sisters joyed to find such curious things
As foundering ships let fall to their domain;
But she cared not for showered coins or rings,
And claimed no share of all that precious rain
Except a marble statue, – some boy-king's,
Or youthful hero's. Its cold face in vain
She gazed at, kissed, and tried with sighs to thaw,
For still the wide eyes stared, and nothing saw.

9

Thereby she set a weeping-willow tree
To droop and mourn. Full dolefully it clung
About the form, and moved continually,
As if it sighed; as if it sometimes wrung
Convulsive fingers in sad reverie.
And ever o'er the light blue sand it hung
A purple shade, which hour by hour the same,
Burnt softly on, like lambent sulphur flame.

10

Soon, for the twilight of that shadow's ring,
The girl forsook the fiery-blossomed grove
And golden-fruited gardens of the King;
Yet not e'en there her eyes reposed; but strove
For glimpses of the sun's far brightening.
Her ear could bear no voice, unless it wove
Tales of the upper world; its tuneful birds
Sweet-odoured blooms; warm meadows; placid herds.

11

Long time before these wonders might be seen
By her, for it was now the year wherein
The eldest sister counted years fifteen.
(Now sea-folk hold it as unthinkable sin
For girls to wander from their sire's demesne
Until a certain year of age they win.)
Rose the first Princess to the waves at last,
And there, in wonderment, a long night passed.

12

Returned, she told her sisters all; and said
Naught was so fine as, from a sandy isle,
To watch a city's lights, white, green, and red,
Pricking the dark for many a twinkling mile.
She caught strange music, and, more strange, the tread
Of crowded men. Then, from some campanile,
Hummed the low voices of the midnight bells,
And bugles fluted in far citadels.

13

A year went; and the second happy maid
Broke the still surface of the evening sea.
The sky was peerless gold; a slow parade
Of violet clouds wheeled westward gorgeously.
Above her, like a white and fluttering braid,
The wild swans winged towards the sun. Then she
Swam westward too; but swift the great ball sank,
Leaving the air all colourless and dank.

14

The third Princess was bold: she made her way
Far up a river, passing vine-clad hills,
And wooded castles all the sunny day.
Oft-times she had to dive or take cool swills
To ease her burning skin. She fain would play
With bathing children; but with terror-shrills
They fled from her; and when dogs barked amain,
She too took fright, and turned to sea again.

15

The fourth remained in mid-seas; whence, said she,
A vast blue bell of glass appeared the vault.
Dim sails she spied; and watched the tireless glee
Of waggish dolphins turning somersault,
And whales a-snorting fountains angrily.
The fifth went up in winter, when like malt
The surge was frothing, and the drifting ice
Shone green as emerald thrones of Paradise.

16

She took a slippery seat on one of these,
And let the winds fan out her long, wet hair.
The near ships scudded on before the breeze
As if alarmed to see her.... Then the air
Fell vaporous-heavy; ocean, ill at ease,
Belched spray; but safe upon her swinging chair,
She laughed to see the vessels roll and leap,
And lightnings zigzag o'er the seething deep.

17

It often happened that the sisters five
Would rise with arms entwined at twilight brown.
O! it was sweet to see them upward drive
Light as the clustered balls of thistledown.
Then would they sing, and singing sometimes strive
To tell storm-tossers not to fear to drown.
But men, who take their voices for the wind,
Must perish ere they reach the sea-folk kind.

18

Said I those linked evening flights were sweet?
Ah! not so unto one!... who stood and gazed
Until the lightnings from the distant beat
Of lashing tails she saw no more; then raised
Her eyes to where the large, pale stars did fleet
Through gliding shadows, and so dreamed amazed
Of shadowy ships; which guessed not the appeal
Of mermaid arms outstretched towards their keel.

Part II

19

So dreamed she through the years; until, oh joy!
The day of her ascension surely came.
Now must the grandame tedious skill employ,
In dressing her as should befit her name.
Though truly all this pomp did but annoy
The Princess: often, with a hurt exclaim,
She would have shaken off the eight large shells
That decked her tail; and ev'n her asphodels.

20

But 'Pride must suffer pain' the dame averred,
And wove the heavy wreath about her brow.
However, all forgotten at the word
'Farewell', she shot up lightsomely enow.
Many a silver bubble she bestirred
To quiver up as up she sped; and now,
Herself a bubble, burst upon the air,
And lost herself within its wonders rare.

21

The sun that moment dipped, but fairy pink
Still flushed the clouds, and long their trailing fringe
Swept on, and waved above the airy brink
Where day was slipping from the earth. A tinge
Curdled the sea, like mingling oil and ink,
Or bloody lymph when witch's flames impinge.
And in the midst of that wide calm, there lay
A large, dark ship, still as a rock, and grey.

22

Only one sail was hoist, for no breeze stirred.
The sailors all about the rigging hung
In easy pose, each like a dozing bird.
Soft music breathed at times, clear voices sung;
And when the shine of eve grew blurred,
Hundreds of lantern fires on high were slung.
Sudden, the dazzle of a rocket-glance!
And on the deck strikes up the merry dance.

23

The mermaid, close beneath, essays to peep
Through the transparent cabin panes; and oft
As she is lifted by the billow-leap,
Espies young human forms, more beauteous-soft
Than she had dreamed; but oh! she holds these cheap
Beside their Prince. Anon he goes aloft,
Whereat a hundred fireworks skyward hiss,
Fright'ning the maid far down the dark abyss.

24

When next she looks, the stars of heaven seem falling;
Suns drizzle sparks, and all is light as day.
So that amid the din and flash appalling,
She clearly sees the glistening pleasure-ray
Gleam from the Prince's eye, as he is calling
For songs, and smiling on his comrades gay.
Why is his smile so sparkling and elate?
Surely his birthday they must celebrate!

25

See how the poesy trembles on his lip
To hear the pining violins, heart torn,
Yearn to the lightsome harps, that o'er them trip,
Like elves about Titania, love-lorn!
Ah, hark, though – in the shrouds above the ship
How envious winds now bodefully 'gin mourn!
The sighing of their wailful harmonies
Hath hushed the lutings and the chaunted glees.

26

It is late. Starry lamps and fierce fusees
Fade out. The stunning guns are dumb. All ears
Hark to grumbling in the heart of the seas.
The ship makes sudden headway; on she steers,
Her canvas spreading to the strengthening breeze;
Till lightning shows a dark shore quickly nears.
Whereat the mariners reef again the sails,
And know they lie at mercy of the gales.

27

The mermaid, clinging to the vessel's side,
Bounding from crest to crest with dizzy swoop,
Fancies they run a right good billow-ride.
The crew, all huddled on the drenching poop,
Think differently. Fresh leaks split gaping-wide;
A mountain-wave bursts o'er a shrieking group,
And sweeps them deep into the deep cold.
The mast falls headlong; water fills the hold;

28

She heels slowly – leans – sinks – O Heaven – she sinks!
With gasp and bubbling groan the brave ship goes,
She and her braver souls.... The nymph but thinks
Of one; and him, just as his eyelids close,
Just as his mouth draws in the first death-drinks,
She finds, upholds, and guides between the floes
Of battling planks and spars of splintering wood.
Then lets the billows bear them where they should.

29

At dawn, the outspent wind sank down as dead;
And gloriously uprist the eastern hues.
They touched the Prince's pallid cheek with red,
And soon with certain life he did infuse.
The nereid kissed him; fondled his fine head,
And smoothed his hair so marred with clammy ooze.
He seemed her statue grown life-sensitive!
She kissed again, and knew that he would live.

30

Now they approached a balmy, sunlit land,
Whose marble mountains, silver-tipped with snow,
Towered o'er a seaboard fringe of citrons bland.
She swam to where a domed portico
Crowned shallow waves: and, passing up the sand,
Laid down her sleeping burden there-below.
Then she drew back, and hid beneath thick foam,
To watch for whoso thitherward might roam.

31

Ere long there issued from that building white,
A crowd of straying girls. Soon one of these
Beheld the prostrate corse; half choked with fright,
She uttered cries; then, falling on her knees,
Besought him speak. He stared, smiled, rose upright.
And with those maidens vanished through the trees.
But no smile sent he to the watching one,
Nor knew he aught of all that she had done.

32

Stricken, as with a wound, she stiffly fell
Into her father's halls; and from that hour,
Her pensiveness increased tenfold. 'What spell',
They asked her, 'cloth thy budding life deflower?
Show us this hidden woe. Thou wilt not tell?
Sister, what sights of ship, or cloud or tower,
Bewitched thee on thy happy day above?'
– Empty request! flow dared she say 'twas Love!

33

Till, after lingering by that quiet beach,
Marking the dazzling snow-caps slowly melt,
Fruits ripen, cornfields mellow, pastures bleach,
And last, the acorn showers begin to pelt,
But seeing nevermore the Prince, her speech
Could hold no more: all, all she felt
And longed for, poured she out in piteous sobs.
And lo! in flooded Hope with glorious throbs!

34

For none among her kindred maids but burned
To help their sister's love, so destitute;
And 'twas not long ere one of them had learned
Where dwelt this Prince of high terrene repute.
So henceforth her fond spirit no more yearned
Unto a vision, once-seen, stark and mute,
But now she held him in her constant sight,
And stayed beneath his casement night by night.

35

He thought himself alone on many a night
While she was close; and gave no noteful heed,
When, in the shadows, murmured ripples slight.
Once, ev'n, as she was hid in bedded reed,
A gust seized hold her silvery veil so light.
But he who saw, must needs the rest instead,
By saying: 'Lo! a swan that spreads its wings!'
– How blind are men to twilight's mystic things!

Part III

36

Much looking and much brooding on the earth.
Desire unsated, daily growing worse,
Begot in her young brain the sudden birth
Of an idea – too strange for her to nurse.
Therefore with fervidness, though feigning mirth,
She brought it to the Queen: 'Sweet dame, rehearse
More and yet more of the world that's dry.
Bears it immortal lives? Or do men die?'

37

So she began, and thus the Queen replied:
'They die, my child, they die. And their life's term
Is shorter than our own. We here abide
Three hundred years; then, like the basest worm,
Dissolve into the foamy ocean-tide.
Now men have brief existence and infirm,
But after, they ascend beyond the stars,
Where tears are not, and naught their rapture mars.'

38

'And why have we no such undying soul?
Oh, I would give my mermaid centuries
For one day human, and Hope's aureole.'
'Think not of that; we of the underseas',
The lady said, 'live happier and more whole
Than men do, with their early grave, disease,
And void despairs. For not all hope as thou,
Nor is Life's crown for every human brow.'

39

'So, at the last, to empty surf I melt;
Drift on the gabbling waves, yet hear no word;
Froth in the soft, warm rains, that fall unfelt;
Fly before whistling winds that pipe unheard
And know no more the place where I have dwelt.'
'And better so! Why, 'less reports have erred,
Many a human life hath envied thine,
And thy long sleep upon the windy brine.'

40

'But is there no way whereby I might find
A spirit like to man's?' 'No way, dear girl,
Unless it chanced some rashling of their kind,
So loved you that you were to him a pearl,
More goodly than his own wide world enshrined,
And wedded you. Nay mark! 'Twould be a churl
Who'd do it. This magnificent tail of yours
Offends their youth. Four limbs, else no men-wooers!

41

'Come, come, be merry! Let us leap about
During the span of years we have to live.
Thou'lt find it long enough, beyond a doubt,
To welcome Death, a blessed lenitive.
Tonight we give a ball: attend this rout;
'Twill stir thy wits: thou'rt too contemplative.'
In radiant revelry soon came the mermen all
And nymphs, and staring fishes, great and small.

42

For ocean hummed with music through and through
And the shades were phosphor-sheened. 'Rejoice! Rejoice!'
The dancers sang; the Princess chanted too,
Delighted; and that night she knew her voice
To be the loveliest and most flawless-true
E'en heard on land or sea. Yet 'twas her choice
To steal away from all the vast applause,
Unto her garden, there from mirth to pause.

43

A bugle sounded through the far dark wave.
'Ah, now', she moaned, 'he surely sails aloft;
He for whose warm, celestial love I crave;
He who could give me in two kisses soft
All joy in life, and all beyond the grave.
Lo! I will venture all for him! What oft
I feared, tonight I'll face. What other help?'
Thereat she 'gan to wind through groves of kelp,

44

Towards the abysmal deserts, where the flood
Spins fierce in spiral phantasies; which, crossed,
Led to a region of warm, bubbling mud,
With slimy weeds and greenery bemossed,
And serpent-polypi, that feed on blood,
And hug old rust, gaunt hulks and treasures lost.
Between their ever-groping arms the lithe girl shot,
A shuddering lightning; then sank safe – on what?

45

The witch's den! Around was filthy quag,
In whose soft mire slow-wallowed water slugs,
Large, fat, and white. There sat the fishy hag,
Beneath her hut of bones. About her dugs
Clung toads; while snakes, with lazy drag,
Wound round her arms, which she, with fulsome hugs,
Embraced and stroked, and fed from her own mouth.
This horror parched the maid's full voice like drouth.

46

'I know, I know why thou art come, fair fool!
Would'st rid thee of thy tail, and wear instead
Two props, according to the earth-folk's rule;
All this that some young prince may love and wed
Thy beauty. So, too, shall ye overrule
High fate, which orders that our dead keep dead,
Not live for aye, as men do fable. Bah!
Hoo-hoo! Buy legs to steal thee wings! Ha-ha!'

47

So loud and so repulsive laughed the witch,
The very reptiles fell upon the ground,
And there lay wriggling. Then 'I'm not so rich',
Quoth she, 'as to refuse a Princess crowned.
Have thy mad will. I'll charm a potion which,
Mark ye! shall give thee legs, straight, white, and sound,
But hurt it must as swords were probing ye.
Drink it at sunrise, sitting near the sea.

48

'All who behold thee in thy changed state
Shall call thee fairest mortal, beauty's queen.
Thine agile, floating elegance of gait
Thou shalt retain; no dancer ever seen
May move so light as thou. But wait, child, wait!
Each step ye take will cost ye pain as keen
As if ye trod on knives. An ye do choose
To bear these pangs, my magic I will use.'

49

'I do,' replied the mermaid; but she shook
As shake the weeds below the surface-storm.
Bethink ye well: thy fish-tail once forsook,
Ye cannot change again from human form,
Nor ever on thy father's Palace look.
And should ye find your Prince not quite so warm,
And fail to win his love – such love that he
Break from his old delights to cleave to thee –

50

'Thou diest: the soul thou reachest after, missed;
Life thrown away. The day he weds his choice
Shall be thy last. Ocean shall be thy cist;
His solemn breast, spurned for a fickle boy's,
Shall nurse thee; shrivelled into spumy mist!
And now, child, pay my dues. I want thy voice.
Needest its tones to charm him, little witch?
Nay, give thy best for this my ichor rich.'

51

'But if thou take my voice, what have I left?'
'Thy buoyancy! Thy matchless mould! Thine eyes!
Come! Let me cut thy tongue, nor think it theft.'
'Take it!... O Prince!... O sweet immortal prize!'
Pale as a faint moon in a stormy cleft
Was her drawn mouth, and wild as winds her sighs.
But from complaint she utterly forbore.
So yielded up her voice, and spake no more.

52

Forthwith the sorceress brought forth her pot,
And having scoured it well with knotted snakes,
Dripped in from her own veins black bloody clot;
Then added poisons, bones, and weird mandrakes;
So that there roamed around the cauldron hot,
Fumes such as rise when roused Etna quakes.
Whilst the loud simmering of that mystic chyle
Droned like the wailings of a crocodile.

53

These spells complete, the mermaid took the juice,
Which seemed as water from the purest fount,
Safe passed the polyps and the whirling sluice
(For the dread charm o'er these was paramount).
Then, hovering o'er her home, she strove to loose
Love's hindering thongs from round her heart. But
'Mount!'
A stronger Love was crying, 'Fast to shore!'
So, in great grief, she slowly 'gan to soar.

54

While yet the sapphire night bedomed the world,
Aground, and 'neath the palace water stair,
Waiting the charmed dawn, she lay upcurled.
In swoon she lay, and she was unaware
How, after break of day, the wavelets purled
About her feet, and licked her ankles bare.
But so it was: the potion of the seer
Had worked its work, and heaven was very near.

Part IV

55

The pang that broke her sleep was quickly spent,
Quenched in a bliss, above all blisses sweet:
None other than the Prince above her bent!
Their earnest eyes like magnet-steels did meet.
She, dropping lids before his gaze intent,
First saw her marble shining limbs complete;
And joyed. But on the instant was amate,
For from her eyes no word could he translate.

56

Much wond'ring why so rich a mouth were mute,
He gently led her towards the stately door.
Even as she foreknew, stabbings acute
Tortured her tread; which willingly she bore,
Although she looked to see the blood out-shoot.
But no stain lay upon the yellow shore.
Only the ribbed sand was soft and sodden,
Molten to jelly, where her soles had trodden.

57

Thus hand in hand with him her beauteous Prince,
Up the broad steps she flew, like wafted bubble.
– And never was she known to cry or wince,
For all the anguish of that secret trouble.
And then they dressed her, as before or since,
Few girls have been. For favour she had double
The other inmates of that courtly place.
And all the land made marvel at her face.

58

The Prince soon found a name to call her by:
Philotis; which was linked on many a lip
With his name, Philo, in a tone full sly.
Greatly he loved to watch her deft feet trip.
For slaves would frisk, and swim, and sprawl and fly,
But tiptoe Lotis almost seemed to slip
Into the air and float upon her arms.
So more the realm was ravished by her charms.

59

Those slaves would also sing, with mimic glee.
Ah, why should young Philotis fall so sad,
When Philo praised them? – 'Twas not jealousy!
But soon a heavier grief than this she had:
Though loved as any fair young child might be,
Though dear as many a lass to one same lad,
She was not the devotion of his life;
He never dreamed to take her as his wife.

60

Long, long she feared to think it; yet 'twas plain;
And every day the certainty increased.
By night, new thoughts would steal upon her brain
Wild as the far-off cry of some strange beast.
And Philo's sweetest laugh became her bane.
And though his merry kisses had not ceased,
She knew her mouth, that never might unclose,
Must seem a blighted bud, a scentless rose.

61

And thus she let her colour fade away,
And languished for cool waters, like a flower.
The more so when her sisters left their play
To watch continually beneath her tower,
And nightly sing how sore was their dismay.
Once, she perceived the King, for one short hour,
And once the aged Queen; but not anear.
They had not risen so for many a year.

62

'My Lotis,' said Prince Philo, one soft eve,
'My parents wish me married, as you know,
And bid me see their choice; but had I leave,
I would not think of this same Princess. No!
I love not an unknown. I had as lieve
Wed thee, Philotis, as commit me so.
For thou resemblest one I love full well,
Who saved my life: a heavenly damosel.

63

When I was wrecked, and cast on foreign shore,
She succoured me; she saved me from the sea.
Twice saw I her; I shall not see her more.
But something of her beauty lives in thee.
Forgive me if too ardently I pore
Upon thy face; kind fate has sent thee me,
And thou hast driven her image from my heart.
Kiss me, Philotis; we must never part.'

64

So when he sailed away in gallant state,
To meet the daughter of a neighbouring king,
Lotis went with him. Then to her he'd prate
Of calms and tempests; fishes; everything
The deep reveals where divers penetrate,
Supposing that she listened wondering.
And sooth she gazed into the waves full hard,
As if they were not dark to her regard.

65

Both day and night her lonely watch she kept,
Leaning above the milky, glistening foam;
Whiles all men save the silent helmsman slept,
And once she thought she saw her ancient home.
And every dusk her sisters rose and wept,
And almost to her side the five upclomb.
By signs she told them she was happy still,
Beloved of men; and nowise treated ill.

66

The ship reached port; and, in magnificence,
Prince Philo waited for his promised bride.
Days did he wait, in nervous indolence.
At last she came. The Prince's eyes flashed wide
With sudden ecstasy; in voice drawn tense
By all the mighty joy of years untried,
And played upon by stroke of present passion,
He chanted (while Philotis' lips grew ashen):

67

''Tis thou! 'Tis thou! Sans whom were I now dead!'
And for a while he could nor think nor say,
But even as her little curly head
Was shut between his shoulders quite away,
So in her being, his soul was buried,
And hidden from the glare of common day.
She was indeed the damsel of the sands!
Well, well may poor Philotis wring her hands!

68

Why should I tell how fine the bridals were,
How many flaming heralds rode the streets,
Or what loud peals went rioting through the air,
Or how the towns were choked with wine and meats,
Since Lotis of these things was not aware?
Forlorn Philotis! Scalding chills and heats,
Visions wherein one face did ever melt,
And, with it, worlds, were all she saw and felt.

69

'Twas so, though still she danced as she was used,
Danced out and far beyond the reach of Art,
For she forgot her feet were sadly bruised.
Her Prince had said: 'You will rejoice, sweetheart,'
So she forgot her soles were sore contused,
Because the sharper pain was at her heart.
Thus the great wedding day came, blazed, and passed,
And fell the night which was to be her last.

70

It found her on his vessel, homeward bound.
Musicians, sailors, revellers, were withdrawn.
The sea was tranquil, heaving without sound.
Already, o'er the east, wan chasms yawn.
The passing billows, weltering mound on mound,
Shone ghastly in the doleful light of dawn.
Then saw she how five mermaids rose all pale,
To save her, if their plan might aught avail.

71

No more their lovely locks streamed out, wind-fanned.
'We gave them to the witch', they said, 'for this,'
And pressed a dagger in her loathful hand.
'Strike deeply at his heart: it cannot miss.
So shalt thou conquer Fate, and Death withstand.
For when his blood shall sprinkle thee, we wis,
Thy feet shall close into a tail once more.
Thus all may be as it hath been before.'

72

So, shrilling, 'Haste!' they sank. And night was spent.
Then she, approaching where the bridegroom slept.
Lifted the scarlet curtain of his tent.
The slumbering pair she saw, and to them crept.
So close they lay, their very curls were blent,
And both her hands beneath his cheek he kept.
Philotis, kneeling, stole her last embrace.
Then turned and watched the sky, a little space.

73

She scanned the coming colour breathlessly,
As 'twere some fateful cauldron, heaving slow.
And now the dull and heavy-clouded sky
Gave forth a steady and increasing glow,
As tarnished lead, that heat doth glorify,
A weird and ruddy brilliancy can throw.
Sudden, like bubble on hot metal seething,
Bulged the great sun. Then ceased Philotis' breathing.

74

Still stood she by the spoiler of her life,
List'ning his dreamy murmurs. What she caught
Was ever one same word: 'Fair wife, sweet wife.'
Ah, She, She only filled his heart and thought!
And Lotis' fingers clutched the raised knife.
But ere the fountain of his blood it sought,
It hurtled back, and splashed along the wave,
And she had leapt into the sea: her grave.

75

The sun passed flaming up his azure path,
And warmed the drift of froth that erst was flesh.
She felt the radiance, and as from a bath,
Uprist into the air, ethereal, fresh.
She had not feathers, as an angel hath,
Nor fairy wings of clear and gauzy mesh;
But yet slid upward, like a lifting mist,
And floated, cloudlike, through heaven's amethyst.

76

Around her, floated spirits fair as she.
No fear she felt of their so perfect form,
Nor of their tongues' angelic melody,
Nor of the numbers of that rosy swarm.
They told her of their office and degree:
To heal the pestilence; to still the storm;
To fan the atmosphere of fiery regions;
Guide honey-bees, and pilot swallow legions.

77

But what they whispered of her after-fate,
The years which this sweet work must see elapse,
Before her final, heavenly estate,
I have not learned. She worketh yet, perhaps;
This evening's sunset may illuminate;
Maybe your garden's tender buds she wraps;
Or breathed the scent into the rose you wear,
Or even now, is smiling by your chair.

78

No more than this knows he that told her tale:
That, looking through the vapours under her,
She saw the ocean, and one lonely sail.
On board was weeping and unwonted stir.
Both Philo and his bride were very pale.
She heard his hushed, half-sobbing voice aver:
'Woe! Woe! The child hath cast herself away!'
And kissed them, gazing on the pearly spray.

Smile, Smile, Smile

Head to limp head, the sunk-eyed wounded scanned
Yesterday's *Mail*; the casualties (typed small)
And (large) Vast Booty from our Latest Haul.
Also, they read of Cheap Homes, not yet planned;
'For,' said the paper, 'when this war is done
The men's first instinct will be making homes.
Meanwhile their foremost need is aerodromes,
It being certain war has just begun.
Peace would do wrong to our undying dead, –
The sons we offered might regret they died
If we got nothing lasting in their stead.
We must be solidly indemnified.
Though all be worthy Victory which all bought.
We rulers sitting in this ancient spot
Would wrong our very selves if we forgot
The greatest glory will be theirs who fought,
Who kept this nation in integrity.'
Nation? – The half-limbed readers did not chafe
But smiled at one another curiously
Like secret men who know their secret safe.
(This is the thing they know and never speak,
That England one by one had fled to France
Not many elsewhere now save under France).
Pictures of these broad smiles appear each week,
And people in whose voice real feeling rings
Say: How they smile! They're happy now, poor things.

The Calls

A dismal fog-hoarse siren howls at dawn.
I watch the man it calls for, pushed and drawn
Backwards and forwards, helpless as a pawn.
        But I'm lazy, and his work's crazy.

Quick treble bells begin at nine o'clock,
Scuttling the schoolboy pulling up his sock,
Scaring the late girl in the inky frock.
        I must be crazy; I learn from the daisy.

Stern bells annoy the rooks and doves at ten.
I watch the verger close the doors, and when
I hear the organ moan the first amen,
        Sing my religion's-same as pigeons'.

A blatant bugle tears my afternoons.
Out clump the clumsy Tommies by platoons,
Trying to keep in step with rag-time tunes,
        But I sit still; I've done my drill.

Gongs hum and buzz like saucepan-lids at dusk,
I see a food-hog whet his gold-filled tusk
To eat less bread, and more luxurious rusk.

Then sometimes late at night my window bumps
From gunnery-practice, till my small heart thumps
And listens for the shell-shrieks and the crumps,
        But that's not all.

For leaning out last midnight on my sill
I heard the sighs of men, that have no skill
To speak of their distress, no, nor the will!
        A voice I know. And this time I must go.

Spring Offensive

Halted against the shade of a last hill,
They fed, and, lying easy, were at ease
And, finding comfortable chests and knees
Carelessly slept.
        But many there stood still
To face the stark, blank sky beyond the ridge,
Knowing their feet had come to the end of the world.
Marvelling they stood, and watched the long grass swirled
By the May breeze, murmurous with wasp and midge,
For though the summer oozed into their veins
Like the injected drug for their bones' pains,
Sharp on their souls hung the imminent line of grass,
Fearfully flashed the sky's mysterious glass.

Hour after hour they ponder the warm field –
And the far valley behind, where the buttercups
Had blessed with gold their slow boots coming up,
Where even the little brambles would not yield,
But clutched and clung to them like sorrowing hands;
They breathe like trees unstirred.

Till like a cold gust thrilled the little word
At which each body and its soul begird
And tighten them for battle. No alarms
Of bugles, no high flags, no clamorous haste –
Only a lift and flare of eyes that faced
The sun, like a friend with whom their love is done.
O larger shone that smile against the sun, –
Mightier than his whose bounty these have spurned.

So, soon they topped the hill, and raced together
Over an open stretch of herb and heather
Exposed. And instantly the whole sky burned
With fury against them; and soft sudden cups
Opened in thousands for their blood; and the green
  slopes
Chasmed and steepened sheer to infinite space.

Of them who running on that last high place
Leapt to swift unseen bullets, or went up
On the hot blast and fury of hell's upsurge,
Or plunged and fell away past this world's verge,
Some say God caught them even before they fell.

But what say such as from existence' brink
Ventured but drave too swift to sink.
The few who rushed in the body to enter hell,
And there out-fiending all its fiends and flames
With superhuman inhumanities,
Long-famous glories, immemorial shames –
And crawling slowly back, have by degrees
Regained cool peaceful air in wonder –
Why speak they not of comrades that went under?

Apologia Pro Poemate Meo

I, too, saw God through mud, –
The mud that cracked on cheeks when wretches smiled.
War brought more glory to their eyes than blood,
And gave their laughs more glee than shakes a child.

Merry it was to laugh there –
Where death becomes absurd and life absurder.
For power was on us as we slashed bones bare
Not to feel sickness or remorse of murder.

I, too, have dropped off Fear –
Behind the barrage, dead as my platoon,
And sailed my spirit surging, light and clear
Past the entanglement where hopes lay strewn;

And witnessed exultation –
Faces that used to curse me, scowl for scowl,
Shine and lift up with passion of oblation,
Seraphic for an hour; though they were foul.

I have made fellowships –
Untold of happy lovers in old song.
For love is not the binding of fair lips
With the soft silk of eyes that look and long,

By Joy, whose ribbon slips, –
But wound with war's hard wire whose stakes are strong;

Bound with the bandage of the arm that drips;
Knit in the webbing of the rifle-thong.

I have perceived much beauty
In the hoarse oaths that kept our courage straight;
Heard music in the silentness of duty;
Found peace where shell-storms spouted reddest
spate.

Nevertheless, except you share
With them in hell the sorrowful dark of hell,
Whose world is but the trembling of a flare,
And heaven but as the highway for a shell,

You shall not hear their mirth:
You shall not come to think them well content
By any jest of mine. These men are worth
Your tears: You are not worth their merriment.

November 1917.

Strange Meeting

It seemed that out of battle I escaped
Down some profound dull tunnel, long since scooped
Through granites which titanic wars had groined.

Yet also there encumbered sleepers groaned,
Too fast in thought or death to be bestirred.
Then, as I probed them, one sprang up, and stared
With piteous recognition in fixed eyes,
Lifting distressful hands, as if to bless.
And by his smile, I knew that sullen hall, –
By his dead smile I knew we stood in Hell.

With a thousand fears that vision's face was grained;
Yet no blood reached there from the upper ground,
And no guns thumped, or down the flues made moan.
'Strange friend,' I said, 'here is no cause to mourn.'
'None,' said that other, 'save the undone years,
The hopelessness. Whatever hope is yours,
Was my life also; I went hunting wild
After the wildest beauty in the world,
Which lies not calm in eyes, or braided hair,
But mocks the steady running of the hour,
And if it grieves, grieves richlier than here.
For by my glee might many men have laughed,
And of my weeping something had been left,
Which must die now. I mean the truth untold,
The pity of war, the pity war distilled.
Now men will go content with what we spoiled.
Or, discontent, boil bloody, and be spilled.
They will be swift with swiftness of the tigress.

None will break ranks, though nations trek from progress.
Courage was mine, and I had mystery;
Wisdom was mine, and I had mastery:
To miss the march of this retreating world
Into vain citadels that are not walled.
Then, when much blood had clogged their chariot-
    wheels,
I would go up and wash them from sweet wells,
Even with truths that lie too deep for taint.
I would have poured my spirit without stint
But not through wounds; not on the cess of war.
Foreheads of men have bled where no wounds were.

'I am the enemy you killed, my friend.
I knew you in this dark: for so you frowned
Yesterday through me as you jabbed and killed.
I parried; but my hands were loath and cold.
Let us sleep now...'

Impressionist

Although his speech ran suavely as a valse
His empty heart gave hollow echoes, false
As ring the vacant city's, late at night.
His narrow eyelids shot suspicious light:

As might the shutters of an evil house.
The more 'good taste' might scavenge, scrub and souse
The alleys of his mind to disembarrass:
The more it left them stony-stark, – like Paris.

And as the erections of his life grew high
And new ambitions piled up fast and thick
So narrower was his knowledge of the sky
So denser was his air with dust of brick.

He valued every man at market price:
Large public parks laid out by legislature
Were his idea and cognisance of Nature.
Neat cemeteries his garden of paradise.

At a Calvary near the Ancre

One ever hangs where shelled roads part.
    In this war He too lost a limb,
But His disciples hide apart;
    And now the Soldiers bear with Him.

Near Golgotha strolls many a priest,
    And in their faces there is pride
That they were flesh-marked by the Beast
    By whom the gentle Christ's denied.

The scribes on all the people shove
    And bawl allegiance to the state,
But they who love the greater love
    Lay down their life; they do not hate.

Happiness

Ever again to breathe pure happiness,
So happy that we gave away our toy?
We smiled at nothings, needing no caress?
Have we not laughed too often since with Joy?
Have we not stolen too strange and sorrowful wrongs
For her hands' pardoning? The sun may cleanse,
And time, and starlight. Life will sing great songs,
And gods will show us pleasures more than men's.

Yet heaven looks smaller than the old doll's-home,
No nestling place is left in bluebell bloom,
And the wide arms of trees have lost their scope.
The former happiness is unreturning:
Boys' griefs are not so grievous as our yearning,
Boys have no sadness sadder than our hope.

A Terre

(Being the philosophy of many soldiers)

Sit on the bed. I'm blind, and three parts shell.
Be careful; can't shake hands now; never shall.
Both arms have mutinied against me, – brutes.
My fingers fidget like ten idle brats.

I tried to peg out soldierly, – no use!
One dies of war like any old disease.
This bandage feels like pennies on my eyes.
I have my medals? – Discs to make eyes close.
My glorious ribbons? – Ripped from my own back
In scarlet shreds. (That's for your poetry book.)

A short life and a merry one, my buck!
We used to say we'd hate to live dead-old, –
Yet now… I'd willingly be puffy, bald,
And patriotic. Buffers catch from boys
At least the jokes hurled at them. I suppose
Little I'd ever teach a son, but hitting,
Shooting, war, hunting, all the arts of hurting.
Well, that's what I learnt, – that, and making money.

Your fifty years ahead seem none too many?
Tell me how long I've got? God! For one year
To help myself to nothing more than air!
One Spring! Is one too good to spare, too long?
Spring wind would work its own way to my lung,
And grow me legs as quick as lilac-shoots.

My servant's lamed, but listen how he shouts!
When I'm lugged out, he'll still be good for that.
Here in this mummy-case, you know, I've thought
How well I might have swept his floors for ever.
I'd ask no night off when the bustle's over,
Enjoying so the dirt. Who's prejudiced
Against a grimed hand when his own's quite dust,
Less live than specks that in the sun-shafts turn,
Less warm than dust that mixes with arms' tan?
I'd love to be a sweep, now, black as Town,
Yes, or a muckman. Must I be his load?

O Life, Life, let me breathe, – a dug-out rat!
Not worse than ours the lives rats lead –
Nosing along at night down some safe rut,
They find a shell-proof home before they rot.
Dead men may envy living mites in cheese,
Or good germs even. Microbes have their joys,
And subdivide, and never come to death.
Certainly flowers have the easiest time on earth.
'I shall be one with nature, herb, and stone,'
Shelley would tell me. Shelley would be stunned:
The dullest Tommy hugs that fancy now.
'Pushing up daisies,' is their creed, you know.

To grain, then, go my fat, to buds my sap,
For all the usefulness there is in soap.
D'you think the Boche will ever stew man-soup?
Some day, no doubt, if...
                                        Friend, be very sure
I shall be better off with plants that share
More peaceably the meadow and the shower.

Soft rains will touch me, – as they could touch once,
And nothing but the sun shall make me ware.
Your guns may crash around me. I'll not hear;
Or, if I wince, I shall not know I wince.

Don't take my soul's poor comfort for your jest.
Soldiers may grow a soul when turned to fronds,
But here the thing's best left at home with friends.

My soul's a little grief, grappling your chest,
To climb your throat on sobs; easily chased
On other sighs and wiped by fresher winds.

Carry my crying spirit till it's weaned
To do without what blood remained these wounds.

The Abyss of War

As bronze may be much beautified
By lying in the dark damp soil,
So men who fade in dust of warfare fade
Fairer, and sorrow blooms their soul.

Like pearls which noble women wear
And, tarnishing, awhile confide
Unto the old salt sea to feed,
Many return more lustrous than they were.

But what of them buried profound,
Buried where we can no more find,
Who [ ]
Lie dark for ever under abysmal war?

Greater Love

Red lips are not so red
    As the stained stones kissed by the English dead.
Kindness of wooed and wooer
Seems shame to their love pure.
O Love, your eyes lose lure
    When I behold eyes blinded in my stead!

Your slender attitude
    Trembles not exquisite like limbs knife-skewed,
Rolling and rolling there
Where God seems not to care;
Till the fierce love they bear
    Cramps them in death's extreme decrepitude.

Your voice sings not so soft, –
    Though even as wind murmuring through raftered
        loft, –
Your dear voice is not dear,
Gentle, and evening clear,
As theirs whom none now hear,
    Now earth has stopped their piteous mouths that
        coughed.

Heart, you were never hot
    Nor large, nor full like hearts made great with shot;
And though your hand be pale,
Paler are all which trail
Your cross through flame and hail:
    Weep, you may weep, for you may touch them not.

But I was Looking at the Permanent Stars

Bugles sang, saddening the evening air,
And bugles answered, sorrowful to hear.

Voices of boys were by the river-side.
Sleep mothered them; and left the twilight sad.
The shadow of the morrow weighed on men.

Voices of old despondency resigned,
Bowed by the shadow of the morrow, slept.

[ ] dying tone
Of receding voices that will not return.
The wailing of the high far-travelling shells
And the deep cursing of the provoking [ ].

The monstrous anger of our taciturn guns.
The majesty of the insults of their mouths.

Page Eglantine

Nay, light me no fire tonight,
    Page Eglantine;
I have no desire tonight
    To drink or dine;
I will suck no briar tonight,
    Nor read no line;
An you be my quire tonight,
    And you my wine.

Mental Cases

Who are these? Why sit they here in twilight?
Wherefore rock they, purgatorial shadows,
Drooping tongues from jaws that slob their relish,
Baring teeth that leer like skulls' tongues wicked?
Stroke on stroke of pain, – but what slow panic,
Gouged these chasms round their fretted sockets?
Ever from their hair and through their hand palms
Misery swelters. Surely we have perished
Sleeping, and walk hell; but who these hellish?

– These are men whose minds the Dead have ravished.
Memory fingers in their hair of murders,
Multitudinous murders they once witnessed.
Wading sloughs of flesh these helpless wander,
Treading blood from lungs that had loved laughter.
Always they must see these things and hear them,
Batter of guns and shatter of flying muscles,
Carnage incomparable and human squander
Rucked too thick for these men's extrication.

Therefore still their eyeballs shrink tormented
Back into their brains, because on their sense
Sunlight seems a bloodsmear; night comes blood-black;
Dawn breaks open like a wound that bleeds afresh.
– Thus their heads wear this hilarious, hideous,
Awful falseness of set-smiling corpses.
– Thus their hands are plucking at each other;
Picking at the rope-knouts of their scourging;
Snatching after us who smote them, brother,
Pawing us who dealt them war and madness.

Antaeus

So neck to stubborn neck, and obstinate knee to knee,
Wrestled those two; and peerless Heracles
Could not prevail, nor get at any vantage...
So those huge hands that, small, had snapped great snakes,
Let slip the writhing of Antaeus' wrists:
Those hero's hands that wrenched the necks of bulls,
Now fumbled round the slim Antaeus' limbs,
Baffled. Then anger swelled in Heracles,
And terribly he grappled broader arms,
And yet more firmly fixed his grasped feet.
And up his back the muscles bulged and shone
Like climbing banks and domes of towering cloud.
And they who watched that wrestling say he laughed,
But no so loud as on Eurystheus of old.

Le Christianisme

So the church Christ was hit and buried
Under its rubbish and its rubble.
In cellars, packed-up saints long serried,
Well out of hearing of our trouble.

One Virgin still immaculate
Smiles on for war to flatter her.
She's halo'd with an old tin hat,
But a piece of hell will batter her.

Who is the god of Canongate?

Who is the god of Canongate?
  I, for I trifle with men and fate.

Art thou high in the heart of London?
  Yea, for I do what is done and undone.

What is thy throne, thou barefoot god?
  All pavements where my feet have trod.

Where is thy shrine, then, little god?
  Up secret stairs men mount unshod.

Say what libation such men fill?
  There lift their lusts and let them spill.

Why do you smell of the moss in Arden?
  If I told you, Sir, your look would harden.

What are you called, I ask your pardon?
  I am called the Flower of Covent Garden.

What shall I pay for you, lily-lad?
  Not all the gold King Solomon had.

How can I buy you, London Flower?
  Buy me for ever, but not for an hour.

When shall I pay you, Violet Eyes?
  With laughter first, and after with sighs.

But you will fade, my delicate bud?
No, there is too much sap in my blood.

Will you not shrink in my shut room?
No, there I'll break into fullest bloom.

The Parable of the Old Man and the Young

So Abram rose, and clave the wood, and went,
And took the fire with him, and a knife.
And as they sojourned both of them together,
Isaac the first-born spake and said, My Father,
Behold the preparations, fire and iron,
But where the lamb for this burnt-offering?
Then Abram bound the youth with belts and straps,
and builded parapets and trenches there,
And stretchèd forth the knife to slay his son.
When lo! an angel called him out of heaven,
Saying, Lay not thy hand upon the lad,
Neither do anything to him. Behold,
A ram, caught in a thicket by its horns;
Offer the Ram of Pride instead of him.

But the old man would not so, but slew his son,
And half the seed of Europe, one by one.

Asleep

Under his helmet, up against his pack,
After so many days of work and waking,
Sleep took him by the brow and laid him back.

There, in the happy no-time of his sleeping,
Death took him by the heart. There heaved a quaking
Of the aborted life within him leaping,
Then chest and sleepy arms once more fell slack.

And soon the slow, stray blood came creeping
From the intruding lead, like ants on track.

Whether his deeper sleep lie shaded by the shaking
Of great wings, and the thoughts that hung the stars,
High-pillowed on calm pillows of God's making,
Above these clouds, these rains, these sleets of lead,
And these winds' scimitars,
– Or whether yet his thin and sodden head
Confuses more and more with the low mould,
His hair being one with the grey grass
Of finished fields, and wire-scrags rusty-old,
Who knows? Who hopes? Who troubles? Let it pass!
He sleeps. He sleeps less tremulous, less cold,
Than we who wake, and waking say Alas!

Beauty

The beautiful, the fair, the elegant,
Is that which pleases us, says Kant,
Without a thought of interest or advantage.

I used to watch men when they spoke of beauty
And measure their enthusiasm. One
An old man, seeing a [   ] setting sun,
Praised it [   ] a certain sense of duty
To the calm evening and his time of life.
I know another man that never says a Beauty
But of a horse; [   ]

Men seldom speak of beauty, beauty as such,
Not even lovers think about it much.
Women of course consider it for hours
In mirrors; [   ]

A shrapnel ball –
Just where the wet skin glistened when he swam –
Like a fully-opened sea-anemone.
We both said 'What a beauty! What a beauty, lad'
I knew that in that flower he saw a hope
Of living on, and seeing again the roses of his home.
Beauty is that which pleases and delights,
Not bringing personal advantage – Kant.
But later on I heard
A canker worked into that crimson flower
And that he sank with it
And laid it with the anemones off Dover.

On a Dream

I leaned, blank-eyed, in lonely thoughtless thought,
Upon the night, athwart my threshold stone;
When there came One with hurried, frightened moan,
With tear-drained eyes, wild hair, and hands distraught,
Who fell about my knees, and swift besought
Help and my love, for she was all alone
For love of me; and from her world out-thrown.
I knew that lovely head; her hands I caught;

For hours I felt her lips warm on my cheek,
As through the vast void of the dark we fled.
For precious hours her limbs in mine were curled,
Until with utter joy I tried to speak:
And lo! I raved with fever on my bed,
And melancholy dawn bestirred the world.

The Chances

I 'mind as how the night before that show
Us five got talkin'; we was in the know.
'Ah well,' says Jimmy, and he's seen some scrappin',
'There ain't no more than five things as can happen, –
You get knocked out; else wounded, bad or cushy;
Scuppered; or nowt except you're feelin' mushy.'

One of us got the knock-out, blown to chops;
One lad was hurt, like, losin' both his props;
And one – to use the word of hypocrites –
Had the misfortune to be took by Fritz.
Now me, I wasn't scratched, praise God Almighty,
Though next time please I'll thank Him for a blighty.
But poor old Jim, he's livin' and he's not;
He reckoned he'd five chances, and he had:
He's wounded, killed, and pris'ner, all the lot,
The flamin' lot all rolled in one. Jim's mad.

The Letter

With B.E.F. Jun 10. Dear Wife,
(Oh blast this pencil. 'Ere, Bill, lend's a knife.)
I'm in the pink at present, dear.
I think the war will end this year.
We don't see much of them square-'eaded 'Uns.
We're out of harm's way, not bad fed.
I'm longing for a taste of your old buns.
(Say, Jimmie, spare's a bite of bread.)
There don't seem much to say just now.
(Yer what? Then don't, yer ruddy cow!
And give us back me cigarette!)
I'll soon be 'ome. You mustn't fret.
My feet's improvin', as I told you of.
We're out in the rest now. Never fear.
(VRACH! By crumbs, but that was near.)
Mother might spare you half a sov.
Kiss Nell and Bert. When me and you –
(Eh? What the 'ell! Stand to? Stand to!
Jim, give's a hand with pack on, lad.
Guh! Christ! I'm hit. Take 'old. Aye, bad.
No, damn your iodine. Jim? 'Ere!
Write my old girl, Jim, there's a dear.)

Conscious

His fingers wake, and flutter; up the bed.
His eyes come open with a pull of will,
Helped by the yellow mayflowers by his head.
The blind-cord drawls across the window-sill...
What a smooth floor the ward has! What a rug!
Who is that talking, somewhere out of sight?
Three flies are creeping round the shiny jug...
'Nurse! Doctor!' – 'Yes, all right, all right.'

But sudden evening blurs and fogs the air.
There seems no time to want a drink of water.
Nurse looks so far away. And here and there
Music and roses burst through crimson slaughter.
He cant remember where he saw blue sky...
The trench is narrower. Cold, he's cold; yet hot –
And there's no light to see the voices by...
There is no time to ask... he knows not what.

Song of Songs

Sing me at dawn but only with your laugh:
Like sprightly Spring that laugheth into leaf;
Like Love, that cannot flute for smiling at Life.

Sing to me only with your speech all day,
As voluble leaflets do. Let viols die.
The least word of your lips is melody.

Sing me at dusk, but only with your sigh;
Like lifting seas it solaceth: breathe so,
All voicelessly, the sense that no songs say.

Sing me at midnight with your murmurous heart;
And let its moaning like a chord be heard
Surging through you and sobbing unsubdued.

Cramped in that Funnelled Hole

Cramped in that funnelled hole, they watched the dawn
Open a jagged rim around; a yawn
Of death's jaws, which had all but swallowed them
Stuck in the bottom of his throat of phlegm.

They were in one of many mouths of Hell
Not seen of seers in visions, only felt
As teeth of traps; when bones and the dead are smelt
Under the mud where long ago they fell
Mixed with the sour sharp odour of the shell.

I Saw His Round Mouth's Crimson

I saw his round mouth's crimson deepen as it fell,
    Like a Sun, in his last deep hour;
Watched the magnificent recession of farewell,
    Clouding, half gleam, half glower,
And a last splendour burn the heavens of his cheek.
    And in his eyes
The cold stars lighting, very old and bleak,
    In different skies.

Elegy in April and September
(jabbered among the trees)

1

Hush, thrush! Hush, missel-thrush, I listen...
I heard the flush of footsteps through the loose leaves,
And a low whistle by the water's brim.

Still! Daffodil! Nay, hail me not so gaily, –
Your gay gold lily daunts me and deceives,
Who follow gleams more golden and more slim.

Look, brook! O run and look, O run!
The vain reeds shook? – Yet search till gray sea heaves,
And I will stray among these fields for him.

Gaze, daisy! Stare through haze and glare,
And mark the hazardous stars all dawns and eves,
For my eye withers, and his star wanes dim.

2

Close, rose, and droop, heliotrope,
And shudder, hope! The shattering winter blows.
Drop, heliotrope, and close, rose...

Mourn, corn, and sigh, rye.
Men garner you, but youth's head lies forlorn.
Sigh, rye, and mourn, corn...

Brood, wood, and muse, yews,
The ways gods use we have not understood.
Muse, yews, and brood, wood...

The Sentry

We'd found an old Boche dug-out, and he knew,
And gave us hell; for shell on frantic shell
Hammered on top, but never quite burst through.
Rain, guttering down in waterfalls of slime,
Kept slush waist-high and rising hour by hour,
Choked up the steps too thick with clay to climb.
What murk of air remained stank old, and sour
With fumes from whizz-bangs, and the smell of men
Who'd lived there years, and left their curse in the den,
If not their corpses...

There we herded from the blast
Of whizz-bangs, but one found our door at last.
Buffeting eyes and breath, snuffing the candles.
And thud! flump! thud! down the steep steps came
thumping
And sploshing in the flood, deluging muck –
The sentry's body; then, his rifle, handles
Of old Boche bombs, and mud in ruck on ruck.
We dredged him up, for dead, until he whined.
'O sir, my eyes – I'm blind – I'm blind, I'm blind!'
Coaxing, I held a flame against his lids
And said if he could see the least blurred light
He was not blind; in time they'd get all right.
'I can't,' he sobbed. Eyeballs, huge-bulged like squids
Watch my dreams still; but I forgot him there
In posting next for duty, and sending a scout
To beg a stretcher somewhere, and flound'ring about
To other posts under the shrieking air.

Those other wretches, how they bled and spewed,
And one who would have drowned himself for good, –
I try not to remember these things now.
Let dread hark back for one word only: how
Half-listening to that sentry's moans and jumps,
And the wild chattering of his broken teeth,
Renewed most horribly whenever crumps
Pummelled the roof and slogged the air beneath –
Through the dense din, I say, we heard him shout
'I see your lights!' – But ours had long gone out.

Inspection

'You! What d'you mean by this?' I rapped.
'You dare come on parade like this?'
'Please, sir, it's—' ''Old yer mouth,' the sergeant snapped.
'I takes 'is name, sir?' – 'Please, and then dismiss.'

Some days 'confined to camp' he got,
For being 'dirty on parade'.
He told me, afterwards, the damnèd spot
Was blood, his own. 'Well, blood is dirt,' I said.

'Blood's dirt,' he laughed, looking away,
Far off to where his wound had bled
And almost merged for ever into clay.
'The world is washing out its stains,' he said.
'It doesn't like our cheeks so red:
Young blood's its great objection.
But when we're duly white-washed, being dead,
The race will bear Field-Marshal God's inspection.'

An Imperial Elegy

Not one corner of a foreign field
But a span as wide as Europe;
An appearance of a titan's grave,
And the length thereof a thousand miles,
It crossed all Europe like a mystic road,
Or as the Spirits' Pathway lieth on the night.
And I heard a voice crying
This is the Path of Glory.

Has Your Soul Sipped

Has your soul sipped
    Of the sweetness of all sweets?
Has it well supped
    But yet hungers and sweats?

I have been witness
    Of a strange sweetness,
All fancy surpassing
    Past all supposing.

Passing the rays
    Of the rubies of morning,
Or the soft rise
    Of the moon; or the meaning
Known to the rose
    Of her mystery and mourning.

Sweeter than nocturnes
    Of the wild nightingale
Or than love's nectar
    After life's gall.

Sweeter than odours
    Of living leaves,
Sweeter than ardours
    Of dying loves.

Sweeter than death
    And dreams hereafter
To one in dearth

Or life and its laughter.
Or the proud wound
The victor wears
Or the last end
Of all wars.

Or the sweet murder
After long guard
Unto the martyr
Smiling at God;

To me was that smile,
Faint as a wan, worn myth,
Faint and exceeding small,
On a boy's murdered mouth.

Though from his throat
The life-tide leaps
There was no threat
On his lips.

But with the bitter blood
And the death-smell
All his life's sweetness bled
Into a smile.

The Dead-Beat

He dropped, – more sullenly than wearily,
Lay stupid like a cod, heavy like meat,
And none of us could kick him to his feet;
Just blinked at my revolver, blearily;
– Didn't appear to know a war was on,
Or see the blasted trench at which he stared.
'I'll do 'em in,' he whined. 'If this hand's spared,
I'll murder them, I will.'

A low voice said,
'It's Blighty, p'raps, he sees; his pluck's all gone,
Dreaming of all the valiant, that *aren't* dead:
Bold uncles, smiling ministerially;
Maybe his brave young wife, getting her fun
In some new home, improved materially.
It's not these stiffs have crazed him; nor the Hun.'

We sent him down at last, out of the way.
Unwounded; – stout lad, too, before that strafe.
Malingering? Stretcher-bearers winked, 'Not half!'

Next day I heard the Doc's well-whiskied laugh:
'That scum you sent last night soon died. Hooray!'

Hospital Barge

Budging the sluggard ripples of the Somme,
A barge round old Cérisy slowly slewed.
Softly her engines down the current screwed,
And chuckled softly with contented hum,
Till fairy tinklings struck their croonings dumb.
The waters rumpling at the stern subdued;
The lock-gate took her bulging amplitude;
Gently from out the gurgling lock she swum.

One reading by that calm bank shaded eyes
To watch her lessening westward quietly.
Then, as she neared the bend, her funnel screamed.
And that long lamentation made him wise
How unto Avalon, in agony,
Kings passed in the dark barge which Merlin dreamed.

Deep Under Turfy Grass

Deep under turfy grass and heavy clay
They laid her bruised body, and the child.
Poor victims of a swift mischance were they,
Adown Death's trapdoor suddenly beguiled.
I, weeping not, as others, but heart-wild,
Affirmed to Heaven that even Love's fierce flame
Must fail beneath the chill of this cold shame.

So I rebelled, scorning and mocking such
As had the ignorant callousness to wed
On altar steps long frozen by the touch
Of stretcher after stretcher of our dead.
Love's blindness is too terrible, I said;
I will go counsel men, and show what bin
The harvest of their homes is gathered in.

But as I spoke, came many children nigh,
Hurrying lightly o'er the village green;
Methought too lightly, for they came to spy
Into their playmate's bed terrene.
They clustered round; some wondered what might mean
Rich-odoured flowers so whelmed in fetid earth;
While some Death's riddle guessed ere that of Birth.

And there stood one Child with them, whose pale brows
Wore beauty like our mother Eves; whom seeing,
I could not choose but undo all my vows,
And cry that it were well that human Being
And Birth and Death should be, just for the freeing
Of one such face from Chaos' murky womb,
For Hell's reprieve is worth not this one bloom.

The Young Soldier

It is not death
Without hereafter
To one in dearth
Of life and its laughter,

Nor the sweet murder
Dealt slow and even
Unto the martyr
Smiling at heaven.

It is the smile
Faint as a [waning] myth,
Faint, and exceeding small
On a boy's murdered mouth.

The Kind Ghosts

She sleeps on soft, last breaths; but no ghost looms
Out of the stillness of her palace wall,
Her wall of boys on boys and dooms on dooms.

She dreams of golden gardens and sweet glooms,
Not marvelling why her roses never fall
Nor what red mouths were torn to make their blooms.

The shades keep down which well might roam her hall.
Quiet their blood lies in her crimson rooms
And she is not afraid of their footfall.

They move not from her tapestries, their pall,
Nor pace her terraces, their hecatombs,
Lest aught she be disturbed, or grieved at all.

Music

I have been urged by earnest violins
    And drunk their mellow sorrows to the slake
Of all my sorrows and my thirsting sins.
    My heart has beaten for a brave drum's sake.
Huge chords have wrought me mighty: I have hurled
    Thuds of gods' thunder. And with old winds
        pondered
Over the curse of this chaotic world, –
    With low lost winds that maundered as they
        wandered.

I have been gay with trivial fifes that laugh;
    And songs more sweet than possible things are
        sweet;
And gongs, and oboes. Yet I guessed not half
    Life's symphony till I had made hearts beat,
And touched Love's body into trembling cries,
    And blown my love's lips into laughs and sighs.

The Next War

War's a joke for me and you,
While we know such dreams are true.
Siegfried Sassoon

Out there, we've walked quite friendly up to Death, –
Sat down and eaten with him, cool and bland, –
Pardoned his spilling mess-tins in our hand.
We've sniffed the green thick odour of his breath, –
Our eyes wept, but our courage didn't writhe.
He's spat at us with bullets and he's coughed
Shrapnel. We chorused when he sang aloft,
We whistled while he shaved us with his scythe.

Oh, Death was never enemy of ours!
We laughed at him, we leagued with him, old chum.
No soldier's paid to kick against His powers.
We laughed, – knowing that better men would come,
And greater wars: when each proud fighter brags
He wars on Death, for lives; not men, for flags.

Storm

His face was charged with beauty as a cloud
    With glimmering lightning. When it shadowed me,
    I shook, and was uneasy as a tree
That draws the brilliant danger, tremulous, bowed.

So must I tempt that face to loose its lightning.
    Great gods, whose beauty is death, will laugh above,
    Who made his beauty lovelier than love.
I shall be bright with their unearthly brightening.

And happier were it if my sap consume;
Glorious will shine the opening of my heart;
The land shall freshen that was under gloom;
What matter if all men cry out and start,
And women hide their faces in their shawl,
At those hilarious thunders of my fall?

A New Heaven (To – On Active Service)

Seeing we never found gay fairyland
(Though still we crouched by bluebells moon by moon)
And missed the tide of Lethe; yet are soon
For that new bridge that leaves old Styx half-spanned;
Nor ever unto Mecca caravanned;
Nor bugled Asgard, skilled in magic rune;
Nor yearned for far Nirvana, the sweet swoon,
And from high Paradise are cursed and banned;

– Let's die home, ferry across the Channel! Thus
Shall we live gods there. Death shall be no sev'rance.
Weary cathedrals light new shrines for us.
To us, rough knees of boys shall ache with rev'rence.
Are not girls' breasts a clear, strong Acropole?
– There our own mothers' tears shall heal us whole.

The Roads Also

The roads also have their wistful rest,
When the weathercocks perch still and roost,
And the looks of men turn kind to clocks
And the trams go empty to their drome.
        The streets also dream their dream.

The old houses muse of the old days
And their fond trees lean on them doze.
On their steps chatter and clatter stops
For the cries of other times hold men
        And they hear the unknown moan.

They remember alien ardours and far futures
And the smiles not seen in happy features.
Their begetters call them from the gutters;
In the gardens unborn child-souls wail,
        And the dead scribble on walls.

Though their own child cry for them in tears,
Women weep but hear no sound upstairs.
They believe in love they had not lived
And passion past the reach of stairs
        To the world's towers or stars.

Unto What Pinnacles

Unto what pinnacles of desperate heights
Do good men climb to seize their good!
What abnegation to all mortal joys,
What vast abstraction from the world is theirs!
O what insane abuses, desperate pangs,
Annihilations of the Self, soul-suicides,
They wreak upon themselves to purchase – God!
A God to guide through these poor temporal days
Their comings, goings, workings of the heart,
Obsess, indeed, their natures utterly;
Meanwhile preparing, as in recompense,
Mansions celestial for their timeless bliss.
And to what end this Holiness; this God
That arrogates their intellect and soul?
To none! Their offered lives are not so grand,
So active, or so sweet as many a one's
That is undedicate, being reason-swayed;
And their sole mission is to drag, entice
And push mankind to those same cloudy crags
Where they first breathed the madness-giving air
That made them feel as angels, that are less than men.

The Show

We have fallen in the dreams the ever-living
Breathe on the tarnished mirror of the world,
And then smooth out with ivory hands and sigh.
W. B. Yeats

My soul looked down from a vague height, with Death,
As unremembering how I rose or why,
And saw a sad land, weak with sweats of dearth,
Gray, cratered like the moon with hollow woe,
And pitted with great pocks and scabs of plagues.

Across its beard, that horror of harsh wire,
There moved thin caterpillars, slowly uncoiled.
It seemed they pushed themselves to be as plugs
Of ditches, where they writhed and shrivelled, killed.

By them had slimy paths been trailed and scraped
Round myriad warts that might be little hills.

From gloom's last dregs these long-strung creatures crept,
And vanished out of dawn down hidden holes.

(And smell came up from those foul openings
As out of mouths, or deep wounds deepening.)

On dithering feet upgathered, more and more,
Brown strings, towards strings of grey, with bristling
spines,
All migrants from green fields, intent on mire.

Those that were grey, of more abundant spawns,
Ramped on the rest and ate them and were eaten.

I saw their bitten backs curve, loop, and straighten.
I watched those agonies curl, lift, and flatten.

Whereat, in terror what the sight might mean,
I reeled and shivered earthward like a feather.

And Death fell with me, like a deepening moan.
And He, picking a manner of worm, which half had hid
Its bruises in the earth, but crawled no further,
Showed me its feet, the feet of many men,
And the fresh-severed head of it, my head.

The City Lights

The city lights along the waterside
Kindled serene as blessèd candleshine.
The fires of western heaven, far and wide,
Rose like the reredos of a mighty shrine.
Slow swung the odorous trees from side to side,
Like censers, twining twilight mist for fume;
And on the mountain, that high altar-tomb,
The sun stood full of wine, blood-sanctified.

Soft, soft as angels mounting starry stairs
The smoke upclomb to space; the while a wind
Sung like an organ voicing many prayers.
I, sliding beads, mine errors to rescind,
Of slowly slipping tears, heard God, who cares,
Ineffable God, give pardon that I sinned.

Six O'Clock in Princes Street

In twos and threes, they have not far to roam,
    Crowds that thread eastward, gay of eyes;
Those seek no further than their quiet home,
    Wives, walking westward, slow and wise.

Neither should I go fooling over clouds,
    Following gleams unsafe, untrue,
And tiring after beauty through star-crowds,
    Dared I go side by side with you;

Or be you in the gutter where you stand,
    Pale rain-flawed phantom of the place,
With news of all the nations in your hand,
    And all their sorrows in your face.

This is the Track

This is the track my life is setting on,
Spacious the spanless way I wend
The blackness of darkness may be held for me?
And barren plunging without end?

Why dare I fear? For other wandering souls
Burn thro' the night of that far bourne.
And they are light unto themselves; and aureoles
Self-radiated there are worn.

And when in after-times we make return
Round solar bounds awhile to run,
They gather many satellites astern
And turn aside the very sun.

All Sounds Have Been as Music

All sounds have been as music to my listening:
    Pacific lamentations of slow bells,
The crunch of boots on blue snow rosy-glistening,
    Shuffle of autumn leaves; and all farewells:

Bugles that sadden all the evening air,
    And country bells clamouring their last appeals
Before [the] music of the evening prayer;
    Bridges, sonorous under carriage wheels.

Gurgle of sluicing surge through hollow rocks,
    The gluttonous lapping of the waves on weeds,
Whisper of grass; the myriad-tinkling flocks,
    The warbling drawl of flutes and shepherds' reeds.

The orchestral noises of October nights
    Blowing [   ] symphonetic storms
Of startled clarions [   ]
    Drums, rumbling and rolling thunderous and [   ].

Thrilling of throstles in the keen blue dawn,
    Bees fumbling and fuming over sainfoin-fields.

Sonnet on Seeing a Piece of our Heavy Artillery Brought into Action

Be slowly lifted up, thou long black arm,
Great Gun towering towards Heaven, about to curse;
Sway steep against them, and for years rehearse
Huge imprecations like a blasting charm!
Reach at that Arrogance which needs thy harm,
And beat it down before its sins grow worse.
Spend our resentment, cannon, – yea, disburse
Our gold in shapes of flame, our breaths in storm.

Yet, for men's sakes whom thy vast malison
Must wither innocent of enmity,
Be not withdrawn, dark arm, the spoilure done,
Safe to the bosom of our prosperity.
But when thy spell be cast complete and whole,
May God curse thee, and cut thee from our soul!

Spells and Incantations

A vague pearl, a wan pearl
You showed me once; I peered through far-gone winters
Until my mind was fog-bound in that gem.

Blue diamonds, cold diamonds
You shook before me, so that out of them
Glittered and glowed vast diamond dawns of spring.

Tiger-eyed rubies, wrathful rubies
You rolled. I watched their hot hearts fling
Flames from each glaring summer of my life.

Quiet amber, mellow amber
You lifted; and behold the whole air rife
With evening, and the auburn autumn cloud.

But pale skin, your pearl skin
Show this to me, and I shall have surprise
Of every snow-lit dawn before it break.

But clear eyes, your fresh eyes
Open; that I may laugh, and lightly take
All air of early April in one hour.

But brown curls, O shadow me with curls,
Full of September mist, half-gleam, half-glower,
And I shall roam warm nights in lands far south.

Training

Not this week nor this month dare I lie down
In languour under lime trees or smooth smile.
Love must not kiss my face pale that is brown.

My lips, parting, shall drink space, mile by mile;
Strong meats be all my hunger; my renown
Be the clean beauty of speed and pride of style.

Cold winds encountered on the racing Down
Shall thrill my heated bareness; but awhile
None else may meet me till I wear my crown.

Uriconium: An Ode

It lieth low near merry England's heart
Like a long-buried sin; and Englishmen
Forget that in its death their sires had part.
And, like a sin, Time lays it bare again
        To tell of races wronged,
And ancient glories suddenly overcast,
And treasures flung to fire and rabble wrath.
        If thou hast ever longed
To lift the gloomy curtain of Time Past,
And spy the secret things that Hades hath,
Here through this riven ground take such a view.
The dust, that fell unnoted as a dew,
Wrapped the dead city's face like mummy-cloth:
All is as was: except for worm and moth.

Since Jove was worshipped under Wrekin's shade
Or Latin phrase was writ in Shropshire stone,
Since Druid chaunts desponded in this glade
Or Tuscan general called that field his own,
        How long ago? How long?
How long since wanderers in the Stretton Hills
Met men of shaggy hair and savage jaw,
        With flint and copper prong,
Aiming behind their dikes and thorny grilles?
        Ah! those were days before the axe and saw,
        Then were the nights when this mid-forest town
        Held breath to hear the wolves come yelping
            down,
        And ponderous bears 'long Severn lifted paw,
        And nuzzling boars ran grunting through the shaw.

Ah me! full fifteen hundred times the wheat
Hath risen, and bowed, and fallen to human hunger
Since those imperial days were made complete.
The weary moon hath waxen old and younger
        These eighteen thousand times
Without a shrine to greet her gentle ray.
And other temples rose; to Power and Pelf,
        And chimed centurial chimes
Until their very bells are worn away.
While King by King lay cold on vaulted shelf
And wars closed wars, and many a Marmion fell,
And dearths and plagues holp sire and son to hell;
And old age stiffened many a lively elf
And many a poet's heart outdrained itself.

I had forgot that so remote an age
Beyond the horizon of our little sight,
Is far from us by no more spanless gauge
Than day and night, succeeding day and night,
        Until I looked on Thee,
Thou ghost of a dead city, or its husk!
But even as we could walk by field and hedge
        Hence to the distant sea
So, by the rote of common dawn and dusk,
We travel back to history's utmost edge.
Yea, when through thy old streets I took my way,
And recked a thousand years as yesterday,
Methought sage fancy wrought a sacrilege
To steal for me such godly privilege!

For here lie remnants from a banquet table –
Oysters and marrow-bones, and seeds of grape –

The statement of whose age must sound a fable;
And Samian jars, whose sheen and flawless shape
Look fresh from potter's mould.
Plasters with Roman finger-marks impressed;
Bracelets that from the warm Italian arm
Might seem to be scarce cold;
And spears – the same that pushed the Cymry west –
Unblunted yet; with tools of forge and farm
Abandoned, as a man in sudden fear
Drops what he holds to help his swift career:
For sudden was Rome's flight, and wild the alarm.
The Saxon shock was like Vesuvius' qualm.

O ye who prate of modern art and craft
Mark well that Gaulish brooch, and test that screw!
Art's fairest buds on antique stem are graft.
Under the sun is nothing wholly new!
At Viricon today
The village anvil rests on Roman base
And in a garden, may be seen a bower
With pillars for its stay
That anciently in basilic had place.
The church's font is but a pagan dower:
A Temple's column, hollowed into this.
So is the glory of our artifice,
Our pleasure and our worship, but the flower
Of Roman custom and of Roman power.

O ye who laugh and, living as if Time
Meant but the twelve hours ticking round your dial,
Find it too short for thee, watch the sublime,
Slow, epochal time-registers awhile,

Which are Antiquities.
O ye who weep and call all your life too long
And moan: Was ever sorrow like to mine?
Muse on the memories
That sad sepulchral stones and ruins prolong.
Here might men drink of wonder like strong wine
And feel ephemeral troubles soothed and curbed.
Yet farmers, wroth to have their laws disturbed,
Are sooner roused for little loss to pine
Than we are moved by mighty woes long syne.

Above this reverend ground, what traveller checks?
Yet cities such as these one time would breed
Apocalyptic visions of world-wrecks.
Let Saxon men return to them, and heed!
They slew and burnt,
But after, prized what Rome had given away
Out of her strength and her prosperity.
Have they yet learnt
The precious truth distilled from Rome's decay?
Ruins! On England's heart press heavily!
For Rome hath left us more than walls and words
And better yet shall leave; and more than herds
Or land or gold gave the Celts to us in fee;
E'en Blood, which makes poets sing and prophets see.

Wild with All Regrets
(Another version of "A Terre")

To Siegfried Sassoon

My arms have mutinied against me – brutes!
My fingers fidget like ten idle brats,
My back's been stiff for hours, damned hours.
Death never gives his squad a Stand-at-ease.
I can't read. There: it's no use. Take your book.
A short life and a merry one, my buck!
We said we'd hate to grow dead old. But now,
Not to live old seems awful: not to renew
My boyhood with my boys, and teach 'em hitting,
Shooting and hunting, – all the arts of hurting!
– Well, that's what I learnt. That, and making money.
Your fifty years in store seem none too many;
But I've five minutes. God! For just two years
To help myself to this good air of yours!
One Spring! Is one too hard to spare? Too long?
Spring air would find its own way to my lung,
And grow me legs as quick as lilac-shoots.

Yes, there's the orderly. He'll change the sheets
When I'm lugged out, oh, couldn't I do that?
Here in this coffin of a bed, I've thought
I'd like to kneel and sweep his floors for ever, –
And ask no nights off when the bustle's over,
For I'd enjoy the dirt; who's prejudiced
Against a grimed hand when his own's quite dust, –
Less live than specks that in the sun-shafts turn?
Dear dust, – in rooms, on roads, on faces' tan!

I'd love to be a sweep's boy, black as Town;
Yes, or a muckman. Must I be his load?
A flea would do. If one chap wasn't bloody,
Or went stone-cold, I'd find another body.

Which I shan't manage now. Unless it's yours.
I shall stay in you, friend, for some few hours.
You'll feel my heavy spirit chill your chest,
And climb your throat on sobs, until it's chased
On sighs, and wiped from off your lips by wind.
I think on your rich breathing, brother, I'll be weaned
To do without what blood remained me from my wound.

5th December 1917.

To the Bitter Sweet-Heart: A Dream

One evening Eros took me by the hand,
And having folded feathers round my head,
Or sleep like feathers, towards a far hope sped,
I groping, for he bade me understand
He would soon fill with Yours my other hand –
But when I heard his singing wings expand
My face fell deeply in his shoulder.
Sweet moons we flew thus, yet I waned not older
But in his exquisiteness I flagged, unmanned
Till, when his wings were drooping to an end
Feeling my empty hand fulfilled with His,
I knew Love gave himself my passion-friend.
So my old quest of you requited is,
Ampler than e'er I asked of your girl's grace.
I shall not ask you more, nor see your face.

With an Identity Disc

If ever I dreamed of my dead name
High in the heart of London, unsurpassed
By Time for ever, and the Fugitive, Fame,
There seeking a long sanctuary at last,

I better that; and recollect with shame
How once I longed to hide it from life's heats
Under those holy cypresses, the same
That shade always the quiet place of Keats,

Now rather thank I God there is no risk
Of gravers scoring it with florid screed,
But let my death be memoried on this disc.
Wear it, sweet friend. Inscribe no date nor deed.
But may thy heart-beat kiss it night and day,
Until the name grow vague and wear away.

The Unreturning

Suddenly night crushed out the day and hurled
Her remnants over cloud-peaks, thunder-walled.
Then fell a stillness such as harks appalled
When far-gone dead return upon the world.

There watched I for the Dead; but no ghost woke.
Each one whom Life exiled I named and called.
But they were all too far, or dumbed, or thralled;
And never one fared back to me or spoke.

Then peered the indefinite unshapen dawn
With vacant gloaming, sad as half-lit minds,
The weak-limned hour when sick men's sighs are drained.
And while I wondered on their being withdrawn,
Gagged by the smothering wing which none unbinds,
I dreaded even a heaven with doors so chained.

O World of Many Worlds

O World of many worlds, O life of lives,
    What centre hast thou? Where am I?
O whither is it thy fierce onrush drives?
    Fight I, or drift; or stand; or fly?

The loud machinery spins, points work in touch;
    Wheels whirl in systems, zone in zone.
Myself having sometime moved with such,
    Would strike a centre of mine own.

Lend hand, O Fate, for I am down, am lost!
    Fainting by violence of the Dance…
Ah thanks, I stand – the floor is crossed,
    And I am where but few advance.

I see men far below me where they swarm…
    (Haply *above* me – be it so!
Does space to compass-points conform,
    And can we say a star stands high or low?)

Not more complex the millions of the stars
    Than are the hearts of mortal brothers;
As far remote as Neptune from small Mars
    Is one man's nature from another's.

But all hold course unalterably fixed;
    They follow destinies foreplanned:
I envy not these lives in their faith unmixed,
    I would not step with such a band.

To be a meteor, fast, eccentric, lone,
    Lawless; in passage through all spheres,
Warning the earth of wider ways unknown
    And rousing men with heavenly fears...

This is the track reserved for my endeavour;
    Spanless the erring way I wend.
Blackness of darkness is my meed for ever?
    And barren plunging without end?

O glorious fear! Those other wandering souls
    High burning through that outer bourne
Are lights unto themselves. Fair aureoles
    Self-radiated these are worn.

And when in after times those stars return
    And strike once more earth's horizon,
They gather many satellites astern,
    For they are greater than this system's Sun.

Shadwell Stair

I am the ghost of Shadwell Stair.
Along the wharves by the water-house,
And through the cavernous slaughter-house,
I am the shadow that walks there.

Yet I have flesh both firm and cool,
And eyes tumultuous as the gems
Of moons and lamps in the full Thames
When dusk sails wavering down the pool.

Shuddering the purple street-arc burns
Where I watch always; from the banks
Dolorously the shipping clanks
And after me a strange tide turns.

I walk till the stars of London wane
And dawn creeps up the Shadwell Stair.
But when the crowing sirens blare
I with another ghost am lain.

A Tear Song

Out of the endless nave
Chorus tremendous,
While the gruff organ gave
Sponses stupendous.

But of a surety
Not one among them
Said the psalms heartfully
Of all that sung them,

Saving one chorister,
Sweet as gay bugles when
Robin the Forester
Rallied his merry men.

Opened his little teeth
Like the round daisy's.
Smiled they for things beneath,
Or Zion's praises?

He sang of friendly bees
Not of the hills that skip,
It was that morning's breeze
Piped on his lip.

But his eyes jewelled were
Of his own singing,
God saw the sparkle there
On his lids clinging.

God the boy's jewel took
    Into His casket,
Flinging the anthem book
    On His waste-basket.

God for his glittering world
    Seeketh our tears.
Prayers show as eyelids pearled.
    God hath no ears.

How Do I Love Thee?

I cannot woo thee as the lion his mate,
With proud parade and fierce prestige of presence;
Nor thy fleet fancy may I captivate
With pastoral attitudes in flowery pleasance;
Nor will I kneeling court thee with sedate
And comfortable plans of husbandhood;
Nor file before thee as a candidate....
I cannot woo thee as a lover would.

To wrest thy hand from rivals, iron-gloved,
Or cheat them by a craft, I am not clever.
But I do love thee even as Shakespeare loved,
Most gently wild, and desperately for ever,
Full-hearted, grave, and manfully in vain,
With thought, high pain, and ever vaster pain.

Impromptu (2)

I have none other thought of peace, but only Thee.
– By which I know thou art not of this world.

One time, the world contained great store of friends,
Mother and Brethren, Teachers, Holy Guides,

All tender to my foolishness; all dear to me;
But this last woe they would not understand.

I once had hopes of heaven, whereon I slept and smiled,
But a cold hand awoke me from that dream.

Only thy youth, fair child, thy beauty, joy, and youth,
Can give me all I want, heart-ease and rest.

Though thou art ignorant of what dark books may hold,
Or darker pages of real human life

Yet thou art not too young, too holy-innocent,
To pity one in pain for human sin.

O Girl, a sole tear, shining on thy cheek for me
More strengthens me than glittering angel-ranks;

Whose glory no eye sees; whose power is never felt,
Whose sinlessness supports no sinful head,

Whose wondrous music never eased a human ear.
– Surely, because they are not, after all.

Ah, well-a-day; seeing my Heaven's empty now,
I would the world were void of all but thee.

Oh, now, unless my face hath set too granite-hard
And hurt thy tender hands to stroke it o'er,

Unless the fires that ever rage behind my eyes,
Hot-sear thy lips in pressing kisses there,

I crave thee, place thy two soft hands upon my cheeks,
So shall long-treasured tears be loosed at last.

Open thy infinite-vast eyes on me –
So shall my life melt out into their depth.

And I shall die away content, without regret;
Content to lose my sense of all for aye,

Simply to live within the memory of thy mind;
And when thy memory fail, to surcease, too.

Who would not part with life if he could surely know
It might lie casketed in such a head?

Purple

Vividly gloomy, with bright darkling glows
Of nebulae and warm, night-shimmering shores!
Stain of full fruits, wines, passions, and the cores
Of all quick hearts! Yet from its deeps there blows
Aroma and romance of violets;
Softness of far land, hazed; pacific lift
Of smoke through quiet trees; and that wild drift
Of smoulder when the flare of evening sets.

Solemn, columnar, thunder-throning cloud
Wears it so stately that therein the King
Stands before men, and lies in death's hand, proud.
Purest, it is the diamond dawn of spring;
And yet the veil of Venus, whose rose skin,
Mauve-marbled, purples Eros' mouth for sacred sin.

Maundy Thursday

Between the brown hands of a server-lad
The silver cross was offered to be kissed.
The men came up, lugubrious, but not sad,
And knelt reluctantly, half-prejudiced.
(And kissing, kissed the emblem of a creed.)
Then mourning women knelt; meek mouths they had,
(And kissed the Body of the Christ indeed.)
Young children came, with eager lips and glad.
(These kissed a silver doll, immensely bright.)
Then I, too, knelt before that acolyte.
Above the crucifix I bent my head:
The Christ was thin, and cold, and very dead:
And yet I bowed, yea, kissed – my lips did cling.
(I kissed the warm live hand that held the thing.)

The Wrestlers

So neck to neck and obstinate knee to knee
Wrestled those two; and peerless Heracles
Could not prevail nor catch at any vantage;
But those huge hands which small had strangled snakes
Let slip the writhing of Antaeas' wrists;
Those clubs of hands that wrenched the necks of bulls
Now fumbled round the slim Antaeas' limbs
Baffled. Then anger swelled in Heracles,
And terribly he grappled broader arms,
And yet more firmly fixed his grasping feet,
And up his back the muscles bulged and shone
Like climbing banks and domes of towering cloud.
Many who watched that wrestling say he laughed, –
But not so loud as on Eurystheus of old,
But that his pantings, seldom loosed, long pent,
Were like the sighs of lions at their meat.
Men say their fettered fury tightened hour by hour,
Until the veins rose tubrous on their brows
And froth flew thickly-shivered from both beards.
As pythons shudder, bridling-in their spite,
So trembled that Antaeas with held strength,
While Heracles, – the thews and cordage of his thighs
Straitened and strained beyond the utmost stretch
From quivering heel to haunch like sweating hawsers –
But only staggered backward. Then his throat
Growled, like a great beast when his meat is touched,
As if he smelt some guile behind Antaeas,
And knew the buttressed bulking of his shoulders
Bore not the mass to move it one thumb's length.
But what it was so helped the man none guessed,

Save Hylas, whom the fawns had once made wise
How earth herself empowered him by her touch,
Gave him the grip and stringency of winter,
And all the ardour of the invincible spring;
How all the blood of June glutted his heart;
And the wild glow of huge autumnal storms
Stirred on his face, and flickered from his eyes;
How too, Poseidon blessed him fatherly
With wafts of vigour from the keen sea waves,
And with the subtle coil of currents –
Strange underflows, that maddened Heracles.
And towards the night they sundered, neither thrown.
Whereat came Hylas running to his friend
With fans, and sponges in a laving-bowl,
And brimmed his lord the beakerful he loved,
Which Heracles took roughly, even from him.
Then spake that other from the place he stood:
'O Heracles, I know thy fights and labours,
What man thou wert, and what thou art become,
The lord of strength, queller of perilous monsters,
Hero of heroes, worthy immortal worship,
But me thou canst not quell. For I, I come
Of Earth, and to my father Poseidon,
Whose strength ye know, and whose displeasure ye know.
Therefore be wise, and try me not again,
But say thou findst me peer, and more than peer.'
But Heracles, of utter weariness,
Was loath to answer, either yea or nay.
And a cruel murmur rankled through the crowd.
Now he whose knees propped up the head of him,
Over his lord's ear swiftly whispered thus:
'If thou could'st lift the man in air – enough.

His feet suck secret virtue of the earth.
Lift him, and buckle him to thy breast, and win.'
Up sprang the son of Perseus deeply laughing
And ere the crimson of his last long clutch
Had faded from that insolent's throat, again
They closed. Then he, the Argonaut,
Remembering how he tore the oaks in Argos,
Bound both his arms about the other's loins
And with a sudden tugging, easily
Rooted him up; and crushed his inmost bones.
Forth to the town he strode, and through the streets,
Bearing the body light as leopard-skins,
And glorious ran the shouting as he strode –
Some say his footfalls made an earthquake there
So that he dropped Antaeas: some say not:
But that he cast him down by Gea's altar
And Gea sent that earthquake for her son,
To rouse him out of death. And lo! he rose,
Alive, and came to Heracles
Who feasted with the people and their King.
And fain would all make place for him
But he would not consent. And Heracles,
Knowing the hate of Hylas for his deeds,
Feasted and slept; and so forgot the man,
And early on the morrow passed with Hylas
Down to the Argo, for the wind was fair.

My Shy Hand

My shy hand shades a hermitage apart, –
        O large enough for thee, and thy brief hours.
Life there is sweeter held than in God's heart,
        Stiller than in the heavens of hollow flowers.

The wine is gladder there than in gold bowls.
        And Time shall not drain thence, nor trouble spill.
Sources between my fingers feed all souls,
        Where thou mayest cool thy lips, and draw thy fill.

Five cushions hath my hand, for reveries;
        And one deep pillow for thy brow's fatigues;
Languor of June all winterlong, and ease
        For ever from the vain untravelled leagues.

Thither your years may gather in from storm,
And Love, that sleepeth there, will keep thee warm.

Nocturne

Now, as the warm approach of honied slumber blurs my
sense,
Before I yield me to th'enchantment of my bed,
God rest all souls in toil and turbulence,
All men a-weary seeking bread;
God rest them all tonight!
Let sleep expunge
The day's monotonous vistas from their sight;
And let them plunge
Deep down the dusky firmament of reverie
And drowse of dreams with me.

Ah! I should drowse away the night most peacefully
But that there toil too many bodies unreposed
Who fain would fall on lethargy;
Too many leaden eyes unclosed;
And aching hands amove
Interminably,
Beneath the light that night will not remove;
Too many brains that rave in dust and steam!
They rave, but cannot dream!

On My Songs

Though unseen Poets, many and many a time,
Have answered me as if they knew my woe,
And it might seem have fashioned so their rime
To be my own soul's cry; easing the flow
Of my dumb tears with language sweet as sobs,
Yet are there days when all these hoards of thought
Hold nothing for me. Not one verse that throbs
Throbs with my heart, or as my brain is fraught.

'Tis then I voice mine own weird reveries:
Low croonings of a motherless child, in gloom
Singing his frightened self to sleep, are these.
One night, if thou shouldst lie in this Sick Room,
Dreading the Dark thou darest not illume,
Listen; my voice may haply lend thee ease.

Perversity

We all love more the Passed and the To Be
Than actual time, and far things more than near.
Perverse we all are somehow; calling dear
Rather the rare than fair. But as for me,
How singular and sad that I should see
More loveliness in Grecian marbles clear
Than modern flesh, to beauty insincere;
Less glory in a man than any tree.

I fall in love with children, elfin fair;
Portraits; dark ladies in dark tales antique;
Or instantaneous faces passed in streets.
I know the dim old gods that never were,
Better than men. One friend I love unique,
But now, thou canst not dream I love thee, Keats!

Soldier's Dream

I dreamed kind Jesus fouled the big-gun gears;
And caused a permanent stoppage in all bolts;
And buckled with a smile Mausers and Colts;
And rusted every bayonet with His tears.

And there were no more bombs, of ours or Theirs,
Not even an old flint-lock, nor even a pikel.
But God was vexed, and gave all power to Michael;
And when I woke he'd seen to our repairs.

The Peril of Love

As men who call on spirits get response
And woo successfully the coy Unseen,
Deeming the thing amusement for the nonce,
But later, when dark spirits intervene
Uncalled, perceive how an invading mind,
Not to be shaken off, compels them serve
Mad promptings; poisons love of life and kind;
Drains force; clogs brain; and flusters nerve:

So I, lightly addressing me to love,
Have found too late love's grave significance.
A fierce infatuation, far above
The zeal for fame or fortune, like a trance,
Exhausts my faculties. I am a prey
Of impulse, the marasmus of decay.

Sonnet

Daily I muse on her; I muse and fret;
And take her little face between each hand;
But spare her – even imagined – kisses yet.
It is because, when first that face I scanned,
It wakened doubts I may no more forget,
And curious dreads I cannot understand.
They reach beyond the fears fond lovers pet,
That faith may change ere death; for they demand:

'What of her after Death? Shall we persist?
Will Death be merciful and keep her whole?'
In wonderment at this, I have not kissed;
And even now methought a whisper stole:
'Hast thou so learned Love's Law, and yet not wist
Her Beauty lives not? How, then, can her Soul?'

To Poesy

A thousand suppliants stand around thy throne,
Stricken with love for thee, O Poesy.
I stand among them, and with them I groan,
And stretch my arms for help. Oh, pity me!
No man (save them thou gav'st the right to ascend
And sit with thee, 'nointing with unction fine,
Calling thyself their servant and their friend)
Has loved thee with a purer love than mine.
For, as thou yieldest thy fair self so free
To Masters not a few, so wayward men
Give half their adoration up to thee,
Beseech another goddess guide their pen,
And with another muse their pleasure take.
Not so with me! I neither cease to love,
Nor am content to love but for the sake
Of passing pleasures caught from thee above.
For some will listen to thy trembling voice
Since in its mournful music warbling low,
Or in its measured chants, or bubbling joys
They hear beloved tunes of long ago.
And some are but enamoured of thy grace
And find it well to kneel to thee, and pray,
Because there oft-times play upon thy face
Smiles of an earthly maiden far away.

Before the eyes of all thou hast the power
To spread Elysium. Gorgeous memories
Of days far distant in the past can flower
Afresh beneath thy touch; yet not for these
Thy mighty spells I love and hymn thy name;

Nor yet because thou know'st the unseen road
Which leads unto the awful halls of Fame,
Where, midst the heapèd honours, thine the load
Most richly prized, of all the crowns the best!
No! not for these I long to win thee, Sweet!
No more is this my fervent, hopeless quest –
To stand among the great ones there, to meet
The bards of old and greet them as my peers.
O impious thought! O I am mad to ask
E'en that their voice may ever reach my ears.

Yet show thou me the task,
That shall, as years advance, give power and skill,
Firm hands; an eye which takes all beauty in,
That I may woo thee thus, if thus thy will.
Ah, gladly would I on such task begin
But that I know this learning must be bought
With gold as well as toil, and gold I lack.
What then? Dost bid me first seek out the Court
Where this world's wretched god, the money-sack,
Doles out his favours to the cringing herd,
There slave for him awhile to earn his pelf?

E'en should I leave him soon, my heart is stirred
With glorious fear and trembles in itself,
When I look forth upon the vasty seas
Of learning to be travelled o'er.
I fain
Would know the hills, the founts, the very trees,
Where sang the Greeks of old. I would have plain
Before my vision, heroes, poets, kings,
Hear their clear accents; then observe where trod

E'en mythic men; yea, next on Hermes' wings
Would mount Olympus and discern each god.

All this to speed my suit with Poesy
Meseems must do; and far, far more than this;
In divers tongues my thoughts must flow out free;
And, in my own tongue, with no word amiss,
For all its writers must be known to me.
My hand must wield the critic's weapons, too,
To save myself, or strike an enemy.
Oh grant that this long training ne'er undo
My simple, ardent love! Throw early dews
Of inspiration oft-times on my brow.
Let them fall suddenly and darkly as thou choose,
Uncertain, fitful as the thunder-drops
Which sprinkle us then cease, to splash once more
Rapidly round, still pausing for long stops,
Not knowing if to vent their heavy store
Upon the parching ground, or wait awhile
Till hasty travelling winds bring increased worth.
But as at last the concentrated pile
Of seething vapours flings its might to earth
In spurts of fire and rain, and to the ground
Flashes its energy, yields up its very soul,
So, midst long triumph-roars of awful sound,
Flash thou thy soul to me at last, and roll
Torrential streams of thought upon my brain,
So give, yea give Thyself to me
At last.
We shall be happy, thou and I. In me
Thou'lt find a jealous guardian of thy charms,
A doting master, leaving all to be

Ever with thee, ever in thine arms.
Forget my youth, forget my ignorance,
Spurn not my lowliness, and lack of friends
Who might help on my progress and perchance
Present me fearless at the throne where bends
Full timidly my lonely being now.
Friends' service would be naught if thine own hand
Uplifted me; do not thine eyes endow
Far brighter wealth than books, and far more grand?
Then come! Come with a rushing impulse swift,
Or draw near slowly, gently, so it be
Never to part.
        Round us the world may drift,
Some with scoffs and frowns, with laughter some:
Their hateful mockery I shall not heed.
How could I feel ashamed to stand with one
Who deigns to stoop and be my life's high meed?
Yet if I would not for its jeering shun
The world, no more would I parade its courts
To change those jeers to applause by showing men
Thy power. Publicity but poorly sorts
My sacred joy, if thou should'st guide my pen.

Loath would I be to show my exceeding bliss
Even to closest friends. But all unseen,
And far from men's gaze would I feel thy kiss;
No witness save the speechless star-lamps keen
When thou stoop'st over me. No eye
But Cynthia's look on us, when through the night
We sit alone, our faces pressing nigh,
Quietly shining in her quiet light.

Stunned by Their Life's Explosion into Love

Stunned by their life's explosion into love
Some men stay deaf and dizzy ever after,
And blindly through the press they grope or shove,
No heed they more or sorrowing or laughter.

And others, having fixed their hope above,
Chastened and maimed by bitter chastity,
Grow to forget spring flowers, and why the dove
Makes music with her fellow, endlessly.

Ah! Pity these were told not that their thirsts
Are slaked not by priest's wine nor lust's outbursts,
But Poesy. These, knowing Verse to be
God's soothest answer to all passion's plea,
And loving beauties' wit and wrought of art,
Might yet have kept a whole and splendid heart.

Long Ages Past

Long ages past in Egypt thou wert worshipped
And thou wert wrought from ivory and beryl.
They brought thee jewels and they brought their slain,
Thy feet were dark with blood of sacrifice.
From dawn to midnight, O my painted idol,
Thou satest smiling, and the noise of killing
Was harp and timbrel in thy pale jade ears:
The livid dead were given thee for toys.

Thou wert a mad slave in a Persian palace,
And the King loved thee for thy furious beauty,
And all men heard thy ravings with a smile
Because thy face was fairer than a flower.
But with a little knife so wantonly
Thou slewest women and thy pining lovers,
And on thy lips the stain of crimson blood,
And on thy brow the pallor of their death.

Thou art the dream beheld by frenzied princes
In smoke of opium – thou art the last fulfilment
Of all the wicked, and of all the beautiful.
We hold thee as a poppy to our mouths,
Finding with thee forgetfulness of God.
Thou art the face reflected in a mirror
Of wild desire, of pain, of bitter pleasure.
The witches shout thy name beneath the moon,
The fires of Hell have held thee in their fangs.

Supposed Confessions of a Second-Rate Sensitive Mind in Dejection

Time was when I have loved the bards whose strains
Saddened the heart, and wrought a heavy mood;
Aye, and my spirit felt a joy to brood
O'er melodies which told of ancient pains.

Lovely the tones when poet's lips have moved
For very mournfulness.... O fair the sight
(As now we see it) of a Spirit bright
Bowed on a southern strand; his work
 approved
Of none; his name despised or else unknown.
O then, how firm and close was his embrace
Unto Despondency! – Her shadowed face,
Methought, how fair! What music in her moan!
Ye, too, have sometimes wished her near;
Loved a chill dampness round the path, and known
Her voice, which like a weary wind and lone,
Fled through the woods with lamentation drear.
But think not, if your life-blood still is warm,
That ye have looked upon Despondency.
Ye have but seen her in another's eye,
As Perseus fearfully beheld the form
Of Gorgon, mirrored in the stilly well.
There may ye guess the beauty of that Head,
The pallor and the mystery – but the Dread
Ye feel not, nor the horror, nor the spell.

But, face to face, she fixed on me her stare:
Woe, woe, my blood has never moved since then;

Down-dragged like corpse in sucking, slimy fen,
I sank to feel the breath of that Despair.

With Autumn mists, and hand in hand with Night,
She came to me. But at the break of day,
Went not again, but stayed, and yet doth stay.
'– O Horror, doth not Pain take note of light
And darkness, – doth he not hold off betimes,
And yield his victim for an hour to Sleep?
Then why dost thou, O Curst, the long night steep
In bloodiness and stains of shadowy crimes?'
She hears my cry, and mutters yet,
'No rest, no rest for thee, O Slave of mine';
Till I do hate myself and would resign
My life to pay a murderer's awful debt.

Out, out to moorlands, from such thoughts I flee
And seek the balm that fair fresh woods distil.
There find I all things in a hush'd thrill
For dread of that grey fiend that walks with me.

She leads me forth, and poisons autumn eves
With hellish scenes; shows me an aged tree
Bending and groaning in its agony
Before a wind tormenting it for leaves;
Spreads out a wild strange sky where towering shapes,
Black and chaotic, choke the sickening day.
Voices moan round; and from the sodden clay
Mist-shrouds crawl up, in token that there gapes
A grave for me at hand.
        Aching with fears
I stumble towards the town, whose distant lights

Glint feebly and go out, and glint again,
Like some retreating ship's unto the ken
Of a lost man, who, sinking, feebly fights
Alone in the wide waste behind.
        The murmuring tone
Of busy streets a moment gladdens me;
But there, too, comes the Spirit secretly;
At feasts I see her shade, and am alone
With thoughts of pain and nothing hear but her.

So that I may not handle a keen knife,
But flashes to the mind a fearful use
That men have made of it, to loose
The heavy-weighted burden of their life
And make an end. But Death is not the end:
No death for such as thou, O Chatterton!
Until the Second Death; and I do shun
The thought that death is misery's friend.
Since my dread Ghost has once a finger laid
Upon my flesh, and left a burning mark;
This mark (saith she) shall fester on, and cark
Will Death draw near, and halting, shade
        O dense
The darkness that shall flood around me then;
Denser the clouds of biting arrows, when
Vile devil-broods to torments bear me hence!

The Imbecile

The imbecile with long light hair, so light
That in the moon it shineth white;
The imbecile with fair long hair, so long
It falleth all her length along,
She nothing knoweth of her wrong.

The imbecile with large green eyes, so clear
Therein her strange soul's deeps appear;
The imbecile with large clear eyes, so green
You see her very dreams between,
Foldeth her angel hands serene.

The Ballad of Many Thorns

A Poet stood in parley
        With Carls a-reaping corn.
Quoth one: 'I curse the Barley,
        More sharp than any thorn.'

'Although thy hand be torn,
        Ill-spoken was thy curse:
I swear thou art forsworn,
        If Thistle wound not worse.'

So groaned a footsore Climber,
        Had scaled the bristly path:
'What thorns, Sir Carl, Sir Rimer,
        Like these the Thistle hath?'

Behold a wan youth ramble
        With bleeding cheeks forlorn,
And moans: 'The wanton bramble,
        It is the keenest thorn.'

Rode by a wounded Warrior
        Deep muttering like a lion:
'Show me the flesh wound sorrier
        Than by the barb of Iron!'

Out laughed a man of folly,
        Much wine had made him thick:
'The jolly, festive Holly
        Deals oft a nasty prick.'

There hung near by a Jesus
With crownèd head for scorn.
'Ah by His brow, who sees us,
Was any like His thorn?'

So sighed a leprous Palmer.
But when he thought afresh:
'Perchance His pain was calmer,
Than this thorn in my flesh.'

Then cried the gentle Poet:
'Not one among ye knows:
The cruelest thorn, I know it,
For having kissed the Rose.'

The Dread of Falling into Naught

Now slows the beat of Summer's dancing pulse;
Her voice has weak and quaverous undertones;
Cold agues in her hectic limbs convulse;
Show palsies creep into her sapless bones.
Ah! is she falling into Death so soon, so soon?

Ev'n so! and now the peerless forest green
Is streaked with silvery pallor of decay.
As a beauteous woman's locks may lose their sheen
Through fearful dreams, and turn too early grey,
So Summer paleth now, and moaneth in her swoon.

The expressions of her once-rich mind, and flowers,
Are feeble-born, else rank unnaturally;
And whoso looks on leafy garden bowers,
Fresh bloodstains every misty morn may see,
Split from her veins by Winter's lance, and conflict-strewn.

My power of life, though youthful, also sinks;
Before my time I bear a hoary head;
And chill airs strike my brow, that blow, methinks,
Straight from the icy cavern of the dead.
Night darkens round; my day shall know no afternoon.

O never mourn, my brothers! well ye know
These crimson stains shall vanish from the trees;
Washed by the precious ointment of the snow.
A little while, and drowsy Earth's disease,
Shall feel the healing quickness of another June.

I, only mourn, because I cannot tell
What spring-renewing wakes the sleep of Men.
I do but know, (ah! this I know too well)
I shall not see the same sweet life again,
Nor the dear Sun, nor stars, nor tender moon.

The Fates

They watch me, those informers to the Fates
Called Fortune, Chance, Necessity, and Death;
Time, in disguise as one who serves and waits,
Eternity as girls of fragrant breath.
I know them. Men and Boys are in their pay,
And those I hold my trustiest friends may prove
Agents of Theirs to take me if I stray
From fatal ordinance. If I move, they move –

Escape? There is one unwatched way; your eyes,
O Beauty! Keep me good that secret gate!
And when the cordon tightens of the spies
Let the close iris of your eyes grow great.
So I'll evade the vice and rack of age
And miss the march of lifetime, stage by stage.

The One Remains

I sometimes think of those pale, perfect faces
My wonder has not looked upon, as yet;
And of those others never to be met;
And often pore I on the secret traces
Left in my heart, of countenances seen,
And lost as soon as seen, – but which mine eye
Remembers as my old home, or the lie
Of landscapes whereupon my windows lean.

And as for those long known and worshipped long,
But now, alas! no longer, and the song
Of voices that have said 'Adieu, we part,'
Their reminiscences would cease my heart,
Except I still hoped find, some time, some place,
All beauty, once for ever, in one face.

The Poet in Pain

Some men sing songs of Pain and scarcely guess
Their import, for they never knew her stress.
And there be other souls that ever lie
Begnawed by seven devils, silent. Aye,
Whose hearts have wept out blood, who not once spake
Of tears. If therefore my remorseless ache
Be needful to proof-test upon my flesh
The thoughts I think, and in words bleeding-fresh
Teach me for speechless sufferers to plain,
I would not quench it. Rather be my part
To write of health with shaking hands, bone-pale,
Of pleasure, having hell in every vein,
Than chant of care from out a careless heart,
To music of the world's eternal wail.

The Swift: An Ode

When the blue has broken
Through the pearly heat
And the grass is woken
By our early feet,
Oh, then to be the Lark! – With all his fun
To pelt my mate with gayest kisses,
And mount to laugh away those blisses
In shaking merriment unto the sun!

When the dark is listening
And the leaves hang still,
While the glow-worms, glistening,
Make the keen stars thrill,
Would I might mourn to one lorn Nightingale
And be the solace of her solitude,
Speaking my doles all clear and unsubdued
And audible to her, the Nightingale.

But when eve shines lowly,
And the light is thinned,
And the moon slides slowly
Down the far-off wind,
Oh, then to be of all the birds the Swift!
To flit through ether, with elves winging,
Drawn up western fires, in frenzy singing,
Along the breeze to lean and poise and drift!

Fine thou art and agile,
O thou perfect bird,

As an arrow fragile
By an Eros whirred;
And like a cross-bow in a Cupid's grasp
Thy wings are ever stretched, for striking ready;
And like young Love thou'rt frantic and unsteady,
And sure as his thine aim, and keen as Love's thy gasp.

Strung in tautest tension
By the lust of speed,
And the mad contention
Of insatiate greed,
Thou suck'st away the intoxicating air,
Trailing a wake of song in trilling bubbles,
Till distance drowns thee. Then thy light wing doubles,
And thou art back, – nay vanished now, Oh where?

Down in sharp declension,
Grazing the low pool;
Up in steep ascension
Where the clouds blow cool;
And there thou sleepest all the luminous night,
Aloft this hurry and this hunger,
Floating with years that knew thee younger,
Without this nest to feed, this death to fight.

Airily sweeping and swinging,
Quivering unstable,
Like a dark butterfly clinging
To the roof-gable,
Art thou not tired of this unceasing round?
Long'st not for rest in mead or bower?

Must lose, as spirits lose, the power
To soar again if once thou come to ground?

Waywardly sliding and slinging,
Speed never slacking,
Easily, recklessly flinging,
Twinkling and tacking;
– Oh, how we envy thee thy lovely swerves!
How covet we thy slim wings' beauty,
Nor guess what stress of need and duty
So bent thy frame to those slim faultless curves.

Dazzlingly swooping and plunging
Into the nest to peep,
Dangerously leaping and lunging –
Hark! how the younglings cheep!
O Swift! If thou art master of the air
Who taught thee! Not the joy of flying
But of thy brood: their throttles' crying
Stung thee to skill whereof men yet despair!

Desperately driving and dashing,
Hissing and shrieking,
Breathlessly hurtling and lashing,
Seeking and seeking,
What knowest thou of grace or dance or song?
Thy cry that ringeth like a lyric,
Is it indeed of joy, a panegyric?
No ecstasy is this. By love's pain it rings strong.

O that I might make me
Pinions like to thine,

Feathers that would take me
Whither I incline!
Yet more thy spirit's tirelessness I crave;
Yet more thy joyous fierce endurance.
If my soul flew with thy assurance,
What fields, what skies to scour! What seas to brave!

The Two Reflections

I seldom look into thy brown eyes, child,
But I behold in them the deep, cool shade
Of summer woods. Hence always, if dismayed
To think how quickly Time hath us beguiled
Of those enchanted days, when forest-wild,
We roamed the copses, and so gaily played;
I feel about me yet the dusky glade,
And June's late light through long lanes, beechen-aisled.
And in the glistening of thy fragrant hair
Sparkles the scented rain that glistened then.
But ah! I see, too, thou being otherwhere,
Thy shadowy eyes in every low-lit glen;
Thy locks in every sun-gilt shower, and there
In those sweet glooms, find sorrow unaware.

To ——

Three rompers run together, hand in hand.
The middle boy stops short, the others hurtle:
What bumps, what shrieks, what laughter turning turtle.
Love, racing between us two, has planned
A sudden mischief: shortly he will stand
And we shall shock. We cannot help but fall;
What matter? Why, it will not hurt at all,
Our youth is supple, and the world is sand.

Better our lips should bruise our eyes, than He,
Rude Love, out-run our breath; you pant, and I,
I cannot run much farther, mind that we
Both laugh with Love; and having tumbled, try
To go forever children, hand in hand.
The sea is rising… and the world is sand.

Winter Song

The browns, the olives, and the yellows died,
And were swept up to heaven; where they glowed
Each dawn and set of sun till Christmastide.
And when the land lay pale for them, pale-snowed,
Fell back, and down the snow-drifts flamed and flowed.

From off your face, into the winds of winter,
The sun-brown and the summer-gold are blowing;
But they shall gleam again with spiritual glinter,
When paler beauty on your brows falls snowing,
And through those snows my looks shall be soft-going.

The End

After the blast of lightning from the east,
    The flourish of loud clouds, the Chariot Throne;
After the drums of time have rolled and ceased,
    And by the bronze west long retreat is blown,
Shall Life renew these bodies? Of a truth,
    All death will he annul, all tears assuage?
Or fill these void veins full again with youth,
    And wash, with an immortal water, age?

When I do ask white Age, he saith not so:
    'My head hangs weighed with snow.'
And when I hearken to the Earth, she saith:
    'My fiery heart shrinks, aching. It is death.
Mine ancient scars shall not be glorified,
Nor my titanic tears, the seas, be dried.'

Index of First Lines